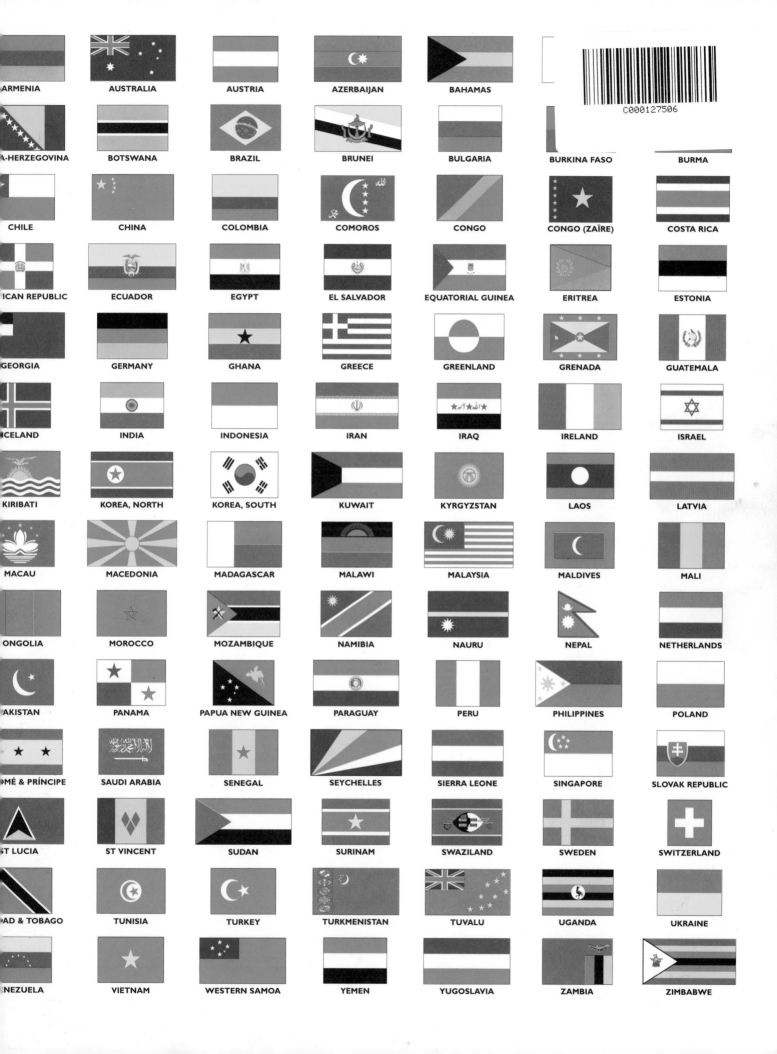

ARMENIA	AUSTRALIA	AUSTRIA	AZERBAIJAN	BAHAMAS
A-HERZEGOVINA	BOTSWANA	BRAZIL	BRUNEI	BULGARIA	BURKINA FASO	BURMA
CHILE	CHINA	COLOMBIA	COMOROS	CONGO	CONGO (ZAÏRE)	COSTA RICA
ICAN REPUBLIC	ECUADOR	EGYPT	EL SALVADOR	EQUATORIAL GUINEA	ERITREA	ESTONIA
GEORGIA	GERMANY	GHANA	GREECE	GREENLAND	GRENADA	GUATEMALA
ICELAND	INDIA	INDONESIA	IRAN	IRAQ	IRELAND	ISRAEL
KIRIBATI	KOREA, NORTH	KOREA, SOUTH	KUWAIT	KYRGYZSTAN	LAOS	LATVIA
MACAU	MACEDONIA	MADAGASCAR	MALAWI	MALAYSIA	MALDIVES	MALI
ONGOLIA	MOROCCO	MOZAMBIQUE	NAMIBIA	NAURU	NEPAL	NETHERLANDS
AKISTAN	PANAMA	PAPUA NEW GUINEA	PARAGUAY	PERU	PHILIPPINES	POLAND
OMÉ & PRÍNCIPE	SAUDI ARABIA	SENEGAL	SEYCHELLES	SIERRA LEONE	SINGAPORE	SLOVAK REPUBLIC
ST LUCIA	ST VINCENT	SUDAN	SURINAM	SWAZILAND	SWEDEN	SWITZERLAND
AD & TOBAGO	TUNISIA	TURKEY	TURKMENISTAN	TUVALU	UGANDA	UKRAINE
NEZUELA	VIETNAM	WESTERN SAMOA	YEMEN	YUGOSLAVIA	ZAMBIA	ZIMBABWE

PHILIP'S

FAMILY
WORLD ATLAS

FAMILY
WORLD ATLAS

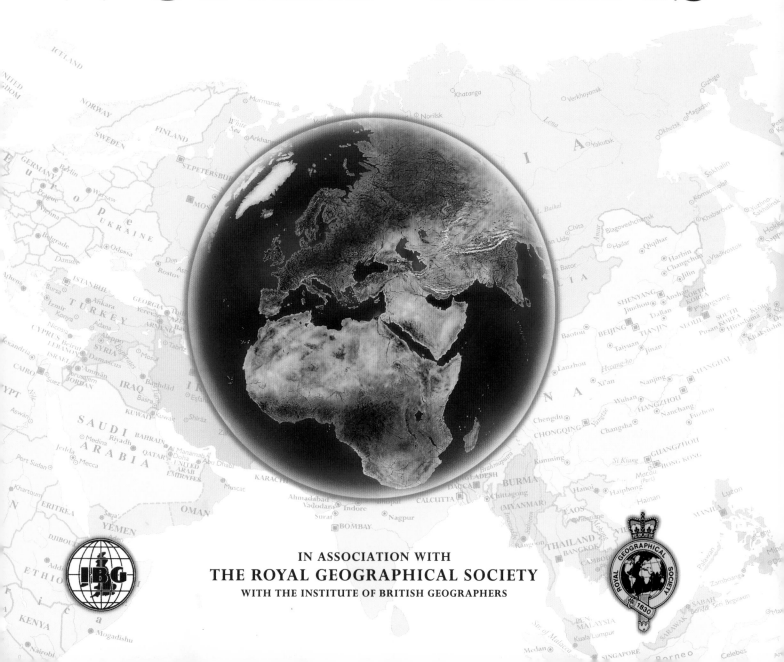

IN ASSOCIATION WITH
THE ROYAL GEOGRAPHICAL SOCIETY
WITH THE INSTITUTE OF BRITISH GEOGRAPHERS

Published in Great Britain in 1999
by George Philip Limited,
a division of Octopus Publishing Group Limited,
2–4 Heron Quays, London E14 4JB

Copyright © 1999 George Philip Limited

Cartography by Philip's

ISBN 0–540–07697–X

A CIP catalogue record for this book is available from the British Library

Printed in China

Contents

World Statistics: Countries

This alphabetical list includes all the countries and territories of the world. If a territory is not independent, then the country it is associated with is named. The area figures give the total area of land, inland water and ice.

The units for areas and populations are thousands. The population figures are 1997 estimates. The annual income is the Gross National Product per capita in US dollars. The figures are the latest available, usually 1995.

COUNTRY/TERRITORY	AREA km² 1,000s	AREA miles² 1,000s	POPULATION 1,000s	CAPITAL	ANNUAL INCOME US $
Afghanistan	652	252	23,000	Kabul	300
Albania	28.8	11.1	3,600	Tirana	670
Algeria	2,382	920	29,300	Algiers	1,600
American Samoa (US)	0.20	0.08	62	Pago Pago	2,600
Andorra	0.45	0.17	75	Andorra-la-Vella	14,000
Angola	1,247	481	11,200	Luanda	410
Anguilla (UK)	0.1	0.04	10	The Valley	6,800
Antigua & Barbuda	0.44	0.17	66	St John's	6,390
Argentina	2,767	1,068	35,400	Buenos Aires	8,030
Armenia	29.8	11.5	3,800	Yerevan	730
Aruba (Netherlands)	0.19	0.07	70	Oranjestad	17,500
Australia	7,687	2,968	18,400	Canberra	18,720
Australian Ant. Terr. (Aus.)	6,120	2,363	0	–	–
Austria	83.9	32.4	8,200	Vienna	26,890
Azerbaijan	86.6	33.4	7,700	Baku	480
Azores (Portugal)	2.2	0.87	238	Ponta Delgada	–
Bahamas	13.9	5.4	280	Nassau	11,940
Bahrain	0.68	0.26	605	Manama	7,840
Bangladesh	144	56	124,000	Dhaka	240
Barbados	0.43	0.17	265	Bridgetown	6,560
Belarus	207.6	80.1	10,500	Minsk	2,070
Belgium	30.5	11.8	10,200	Brussels	24,710
Belize	23	8.9	228	Belmopan	2,630
Benin	113	43	5,800	Porto-Novo	370
Bermuda (UK)	0.05	0.02	65	Hamilton	27,000
Bhutan	47	18.1	1,790	Thimphu	420
Bolivia	1,099	424	7,700	La Paz/Sucre	800
Bosnia-Herzegovina	51	20	3,600	Sarajevo	2,600
Botswana	582	225	1,500	Gaborone	3,020
Brazil	8,512	3,286	159,500	Brasília	3,640
Brunei	5.8	2.2	300	Bandar Seri Begawan	14,500
Bulgaria	111	43	8,600	Sofia	1,330
Burkina Faso	274	106	10,900	Ouagadougou	230
Burma (= Myanmar)	677	261	47,500	Rangoon	1,000
Burundi	27.8	10.7	6,300	Bujumbura	160
Cambodia	181	70	10,500	Phnom Penh	270
Cameroon	475	184	13,800	Yaoundé	650
Canada	9,976	3,852	30,200	Ottawa	19,380
Canary Is. (Spain)	7.3	2.8	1,494	Las Palmas/Santa Cruz	–
Cape Verde Is.	4	1.6	410	Praia	960
Cayman Is. (UK)	0.26	0.10	35	George Town	20,000
Central African Republic	623	241	3,400	Bangui	340
Chad	1,284	496	6,800	Ndjaména	180
Chatham Is. (NZ)	0.96	0.37	0.05	Waitangi	—
Chile	757	292	14,700	Santiago	4,160
China	9,597	3,705	1,210,000	Beijing	620
Christmas Is. (Australia)	0.14	0.05	2	The Settlement	–
Cocos (Keeling) Is. (Aus.)	0.01	0.005	1	West Island	–
Colombia	1,139	440	35,900	Bogotá	1,910
Comoros	2.2	0.86	630	Moroni	470
Congo	342	132	2,700	Brazzaville	680
Congo (= Zaïre)	2,345	905	47,200	Kinshasa	120
Cook Is. (NZ)	0.24	0.09	20	Avarua	900
Costa Rica	51.1	19.7	3,500	San José	2,610
Croatia	56.5	21.8	4,900	Zagreb	3,250
Cuba	111	43	11,300	Havana	1,250
Cyprus	9.3	3.6	800	Nicosia	11,500
Czech Republic	78.9	30.4	10,500	Prague	3,870
Denmark	43.1	16.6	5,400	Copenhagen	29,890
Djibouti	23.2	9	650	Djibouti	1,000
Dominica	0.75	0.29	78	Roseau	2,990
Dominican Republic	48.7	18.8	8,200	Santo Domingo	1,460
Ecuador	284	109	11,800	Quito	1,390
Egypt	1,001	387	63,000	Cairo	790
El Salvador	21	8.1	6,000	San Salvador	1,610
Equatorial Guinea	28.1	10.8	420	Malabo	380
Eritrea	94	36	3,500	Asmara	500
Estonia	44.7	17.3	1,500	Tallinn	2,860
Ethiopia	1,128	436	58,500	Addis Ababa	100
Falkland Is. (UK)	12.2	4.7	2	Stanley	–
Faroe Is. (Denmark)	1.4	0.54	45	Tórshavn	23,660
Fiji	18.3	7.1	800	Suva	2,440
Finland	338	131	5,200	Helsinki	20,580
France	552	213	58,800	Paris	24,990
French Guiana (France)	90	34.7	155	Cayenne	6,500
French Polynesia (France)	4	1.5	226	Papeete	7,500
Gabon	268	103	1,200	Libreville	3,490
Gambia, The	11.3	4.4	1,200	Banjul	320
Georgia	69.7	26.9	5,500	Tbilisi	440
Germany	357	138	82,300	Berlin/Bonn	27,510
Ghana	239	92	18,100	Accra	390
Gibraltar (UK)	0.007	0.003	28	Gibraltar Town	5,000
Greece	132	51	10,600	Athens	8,210
Greenland (Denmark)	2,176	840	57	Nuuk (Godthåb)	9,000
Grenada	0.34	0.13	99	St George's	2,980
Guadeloupe (France)	1.7	0.66	440	Basse-Terre	9,500
Guam (US)	0.55	0.21	161	Agana	6,000
Guatemala	109	42	11,300	Guatemala City	1,340
Guinea	246	95	7,500	Conakry	550
Guinea-Bissau	36.1	13.9	1,200	Bissau	250
Guyana	215	83	820	Georgetown	590
Haiti	27.8	10.7	7,400	Port-au-Prince	250
Honduras	112	43	6,300	Tegucigalpa	600
Hong Kong (China)	1.1	0.40	6,500	–	22,990
Hungary	93	35.9	10,200	Budapest	4,120
Iceland	103	40	275	Reykjavik	24,950
India	3,288	1,269	980,000	New Delhi	340
Indonesia	1,905	735	203,500	Jakarta	980
Iran	1,648	636	69,500	Tehran	4,800
Iraq	438	169	22,500	Baghdad	1,800
Ireland	70.3	27.1	3,600	Dublin	14,710
Israel	27	10.3	5,900	Jerusalem	15,920
Italy	301	116	57,800	Rome	19,020
Ivory Coast	322	125	15,100	Yamoussoukro	660
Jamaica	11	4.2	2,600	Kingston	1,510
Jan Mayen Is. (Norway)	0.38	0.15	0.06	–	–
Japan	378	146	125,900	Tokyo	39,640
Johnston Is. (US)	0.002	0.0009	1	–	–
Jordan	89.2	34.4	5,600	Amman	1,510
Kazakstan	2,717	1,049	17,000	Astana	1,330
Kenya	580	224	31,900	Nairobi	280
Kerguelen Is. (France)	7.2	2.8	0.7	–	–
Kermadec Is. (NZ)	0.03	0.01	0.1	–	–
Kiribati	0.72	0.28	85	Tarawa	710
Korea, North	121	47	24,500	Pyŏngyang	1,000
Korea, South	99	38.2	46,100	Seoul	9,700
Kuwait	17.8	6.9	2,050	Kuwait City	17,390
Kyrgyzstan	198.5	76.6	4,700	Bishkek	700

COUNTRY/TERRITORY	AREA km² 1,000s	AREA miles² 1,000s	POPULATION 1,000s	CAPITAL	ANNUAL INCOME US $
Laos	237	91	5,200	Vientiane	350
Latvia	65	25	2,500	Riga	2,270
Lebanon	10.4	4	3,200	Beirut	2,660
Lesotho	30.4	11.7	2,100	Maseru	770
Liberia	111	43	3,000	Monrovia	850
Libya	1,760	679	5,500	Tripoli	7,000
Liechtenstein	0.16	0.06	32	Vaduz	33,500
Lithuania	65.2	25.2	3,700	Vilnius	1,900
Luxembourg	2.6	1	400	Luxembourg	41,210
Macau	0.02	0.006	450	Macau	7,500
Macedonia	25.7	9.9	2,200	Skopje	860
Madagascar	587	227	15,500	Antananarivo	230
Madeira (Portugal)	0.81	0.31	253	Funchal	–
Malawi	118	46	10,300	Lilongwe	170
Malaysia	330	127	20,900	Kuala Lumpur	3,890
Maldives	0.30	0.12	275	Malé	990
Mali	1,240	479	11,000	Bamako	250
Malta	0.32	0.12	400	Valletta	11,000
Marshall Is.	0.18	0.07	60	Dalap-Uliga-Darrit	1,500
Martinique (France)	1.1	0.42	405	Fort-de-France	10,000
Mauritania	1,030	412	2,400	Nouakchott	460
Mauritius	2.0	0.72	1,200	Port Louis	3,380
Mayotte (France)	0.37	0.14	105	Mamoundzou	1,430
Mexico	1,958	756	97,400	Mexico City	3,320
Micronesia, Fed. States of	0.70	0.27	127	Palikir	1,560
Midway Is. (US)	0.005	0.002	2	–	–
Moldova	33.7	13	4,500	Chişinău	920
Monaco	0.002	0.0001	33	Monaco	16,000
Mongolia	1,567	605	2,500	Ulan Bator	310
Montserrat (UK)	0.10	0.04	12	Plymouth	4,500
Morocco	447	172	28,100	Rabat	1,110
Mozambique	802	309	19,100	Maputo	80
Namibia	825	318	1,700	Windhoek	2,000
Nauru	0.02	0.008	12	Yaren District	10,000
Nepal	141	54	22,100	Katmandu	200
Netherlands	41.5	16	15,900	Amsterdam/The Hague	24,000
Neths Antilles (Neths)	0.99	0.38	210	Willemstad	10,500
New Caledonia (France)	18.6	7.2	192	Nouméa	16,000
New Zealand	269	104	3,700	Wellington	14,340
Nicaragua	130	50	4,600	Managua	380
Niger	1,267	489	9,700	Niamey	220
Nigeria	924	357	118,000	Abuja	260
Niue (NZ)	0.26	0.10	2	Alofi	–
Norfolk Is. (Australia)	0.03	0.01	2	Kingston	–
Northern Mariana Is. (US)	0.48	0.18	50	Saipan	11,500
Norway	324	125	4,400	Oslo	31,250
Oman	212	82	2,400	Muscat	4,820
Pakistan	796	307	136,000	Islamabad	460
Palau	0.46	0.18	17	Koror	2,260
Panama	77.1	29.8	2,700	Panama City	2,750
Papua New Guinea	463	179	4,400	Port Moresby	1,160
Paraguay	407	157	5,200	Asunción	1,690
Peru	1,285	496	24,500	Lima	2,310
Philippines	300	116	73,500	Manila	1,050
Pitcairn Is. (UK)	0.03	0.01	0.05	Adamstown	–
Poland	313	121	38,800	Warsaw	2,790
Portugal	92.4	35.7	10,100	Lisbon	9,740
Puerto Rico (US)	9	3.5	3,800	San Juan	7,500
Qatar	11	4.2	620	Doha	11,600
Réunion (France)	2.5	0.97	680	Saint-Denis	4,500
Romania	238	92	22,600	Bucharest	1,480
Russia	17,075	6,592	147,800	Moscow	2,240
Rwanda	26.3	10.2	7,000	Kigali	180

COUNTRY/TERRITORY	AREA km² 1,000s	AREA miles² 1,000s	POPULATION 1,000s	CAPITAL	ANNUAL INCOME US $
St Helena (UK)	0.12	0.05	6	Jamestown	–
St Kitts & Nevis	0.36	0.14	42	Basseterre	4,470
St Lucia	0.62	0.24	150	Castries	3,370
St Pierre & Miquelon (France)	0.24	0.09	7	Saint Pierre	–
St Vincent & Grenadines	0.39	0.15	114	Kingstown	2,280
San Marino	0.06	0.02	26	San Marino	20,000
São Tomé & Príncipe	0.96	0.37	135	São Tomé	350
Saudi Arabia	2,150	830	19,100	Riyadh	7,040
Senegal	197	76	8,900	Dakar	600
Seychelles	0.46	0.18	78	Victoria	6,370
Sierra Leone	71.7	27.7	4,600	Freetown	180
Singapore	0.62	0.24	3,200	Singapore	26,730
Slovak Republic	49	18.9	5,400	Bratislava	2,950
Slovenia	20.3	7.8	2,000	Ljubljana	8,200
Solomon Is.	28.9	11.2	410	Honiara	910
Somalia	638	246	9,900	Mogadishu	500
South Africa	1,220	471	42,300	C. Town/Pretoria/Bloem.	3,160
Spain	505	195	39,300	Madrid	13,580
Sri Lanka	65.6	25.3	18,700	Colombo	700
Sudan	2,506	967	31,000	Khartoum	750
Surinam	163	63	500	Paramaribo	880
Svalbard (Norway)	62.9	24.3	4	Longyearbyen	–
Swaziland	17.4	6.7	1,000	Mbabane	1,170
Sweden	450	174	8,900	Stockholm	23,750
Switzerland	41.3	15.9	7,100	Bern	40,630
Syria	185	71	15,300	Damascus	1,120
Taiwan	36	13.9	21,700	Taipei	12,000
Tajikistan	143.1	55.2	6,000	Dushanbe	340
Tanzania	945	365	31,200	Dodoma	120
Thailand	513	198	60,800	Bangkok	2,740
Togo	56.8	21.9	4,500	Lomé	310
Tokelau (NZ)	0.01	0.005	2	Nukunonu	–
Tonga	0.75	0.29	107	Nuku'alofa	1,610
Trinidad & Tobago	5.1	2	1,300	Port of Spain	3,770
Tristan da Cunha (UK)	0.11	0.04	0.33	Edinburgh	–
Tunisia	164	63	9,200	Tunis	1,820
Turkey	779	301	63,500	Ankara	2,780
Turkmenistan	488.1	188.5	4,800	Ashkhabad	920
Turks & Caicos Is. (UK)	0.43	0.17	15	Cockburn Town	5,000
Tuvalu	0.03	0.01	10	Fongafale	600
Uganda	236	91	20,800	Kampala	240
Ukraine	603.7	233.1	51,500	Kiev	1,630
United Arab Emirates	83.6	32.3	2,400	Abu Dhabi	17,400
United Kingdom	243.3	94	58,600	London	18,700
United States of America	9,373	3,619	268,000	Washington, DC	26,980
Uruguay	177	68	3,300	Montevideo	5,170
Uzbekistan	447.4	172.7	23,800	Tashkent	970
Vanuatu	12.2	4.7	175	Port-Vila	1,200
Vatican City	0.0004	0.0002	1	–	–
Venezuela	912	352	22,500	Caracas	3,020
Vietnam	332	127	77,100	Hanoi	240
Virgin Is. (UK)	0.15	0.06	13	Road Town	–
Virgin Is. (US)	0.34	0.13	105	Charlotte Amalie	12,000
Wake Is.	0.008	0.003	0.30	–	–
Wallis & Futuna Is. (Fr.)	0.20	0.08	15	Mata-Utu	–
Western Sahara	266	103	280	El Aaiún	980
Western Samoa	2.8	1.1	175	Apia	1,120
Yemen	528	204	16,500	Sana	260
Yugoslavia	102.3	39.5	10,500	Belgrade	1,400
Zambia	753	291	9,500	Lusaka	400
Zimbabwe	391	151	12,100	Harare	540

World Statistics: Cities

This list shows the principal cities with more than 500,000 inhabitants (for China and India only cities with more than 1 million inhabitants are included). The figures are taken from the most recent census or estimate, and are the population of the metropolitan area, e.g. greater New York, Mexico or Paris. All the figures are in thousands. Local name forms have been used for the smaller cities (e.g. Kraków).

AFGHANISTAN
Kabul 1,565
ALGERIA
Algiers 1,722
Oran 664
ANGOLA
Luanda 2,250
ARGENTINA
Buenos Aires 10,990
Córdoba 1,198
Rosario 1,096
Mendoza 775
La Plata 640
San Miguel de
Tucumán 622
Mar del Plata 520
ARMENIA
Yerevan 1,226
AUSTRALIA
Sydney 3,713
Melbourne 3,189
Brisbane 1,422
Perth 1,221
Adelaide 1,071
AUSTRIA
Vienna 1,560
AZERBAIJAN
Baku 1,081
BANGLADESH
Dhaka 7,832
Chittagong 2,041
Khulna 877
Rajshahi 517
BELARUS
Minsk 1,700
Homyel 512
BELGIUM
Brussels 952
BENIN
Cotonou 537
BOLIVIA
La Paz 1,126
Santa Cruz 767
BOSNIA-HERZEGOVINA
Sarajevo 526
BRAZIL
São Paulo 16,417
Rio de Janeiro 9,888
Salvador 2,056
Belo Horizonte 2,049
Fortaleza 1,758
Brasília 1,596
Curitiba 1,290
Recife 1,290
Nova Iguaçu 1,286
Pôrto Alegre 1,263
Belém 1,246
Manaus 1,011
Goiânia 921
Campinas 846
Guarulhos 781
São Gonçalo 748
São Luís 696
Duque de Caxias 665
Maceió 628
Santo André 614
Natal 607
Teresina 598
São Bernado de
Campo 565
Osasco 563
Campo Grande 526
BULGARIA
Sofia 1,117
BURKINA FASO
Ouagadougou 690
BURMA (MYANMAR)
Rangoon 2,513
Mandalay 533

CAMBODIA
Phnom Penh 920
CAMEROON
Douala 884
Yaoundé 750
CANADA
Toronto 4,264
Montréal 3,327
Vancouver 1,832
Ottawa-Hull 1,010
Edmonton 863
Calgary 822
Québec 672
Winnipeg 667
Hamilton 624
CENTRAL AFRICAN REP.
Bangui 706
CHAD
Ndjaména 530
CHILE
Santiago 5,077
CHINA
Shanghai 15,082
Beijing 12,362
Tianjin 10,687
Hong Kong (SAR)* 6,205
Chongqing 3,870
Shenyang 3,762
Wuhan 3,520
Guangzhou 3,114
Harbin 2,505
Nanjing 2,211
Xi'an 2,115
Chengdu 1,933
Dalian 1,855
Changchun 1,810
Jinan 1,660
Taiyuan 1,642
Qingdao 1,584
Fuzhou, Fujian 1,380
Zibo 1,346
Zhengzhou 1,324
Lanzhou 1,296
Anshan 1,252
Fushun 1,246
Kunming 1,242
Changsha 1,198
Hangzhou 1,185
Nanchang 1,169
Shijiazhuang 1,159
Guiyang 1,131
Ürümqi 1,130
Jilin 1,118
Hefei 1,110
Tangshan 1,110
Baotou 1,033
COLOMBIA
Bogotá 5,026
Cali 1,719
Medellin 1,621
Barranquilla 1,064
Cartagena 746
CONGO
Brazzaville 938
Pointe-Noire 576
CONGO (= ZAÏRE)
Kinshasa 3,804
Lubumbashi 739
Mbuji-Mayi 613
Kolwezi 544
COSTA RICA
San José 1,186
CROATIA
Zagreb 931
CUBA
Havana 2,143
CZECH REPUBLIC
Prague 1,217
DENMARK
Copenhagen 1,353

DOMINICAN REP.
Santo Domingo 2,135
Santiago 691
ECUADOR
Guayaquil 1,925
Quito 1,444
EGYPT
Cairo 9,656
Alexandria 3,380
El Gîza 2,144
Shubra el Kheima 834
EL SALVADOR
San Salvador 1,522
ETHIOPIA
Addis Ababa 2,316
FINLAND
Helsinki 525
FRANCE
Paris 9,469
Lyon 1,262
Marseille 1,087
Lille 959
Bordeaux 696
Toulouse 650
Nice 516
GEORGIA
Tbilisi 1,279
GERMANY
Berlin 3,472
Hamburg 1,706
Munich 1,245
Cologne 964
Frankfurt 652
Essen 618
Dortmund 601
Stuttgart 588
Düsseldorf 573
Bremen 549
Duisburg 536
Hanover 526
GHANA
Accra 1,781
Kumasi 540
GREECE
Athens 3,097
GUATEMALA
Guatemala 1,814
GUINEA
Conakry 1,508
HAITI
Port-au-Prince 1,402
HONDURAS
Tegucigalpa 739
HUNGARY
Budapest 1,909
INDIA
Bombay
(Mumbai) 15,093
Calcutta 11,673
Delhi 9,882
Madras (Chennai) 5,361
Hyderabad 4,280
Bangalore 4,087
Ahmadabad 3,298
Pune 2,485
Kanpur 2,111
Nagpur 1,661
Lucknow 1,642
Surat 1,517
Jaipur 1,514
Coimbatore 1,136
Vadodara 1,115
Indore 1,104
Patna 1,099
Madurai 1,094
Bhopal 1,064
Vishakhapatnam 1,052
Varanasi 1,026
Ludhiana 1,012
INDONESIA
Jakarta 11,500

Surabaya 2,701
Bandung 2,368
Medan 1,910
Semarang 1,366
Palembang 1,352
Ujung Pandang 1,092
Bandar Lampung 832
Malang 763
IRAN
Tehran 6,750
Mashhad 1,964
Esfahan 1,221
Tabriz 1,166
Shiraz 1,043
Ahvaz 828
Qom 780
Bakhtaran 666
Karaj 588
IRAQ
Baghdad 3,841
Diyala 961
As Sulaymaniyah 952
Arbil 770
Al Mawsil 644
Kadhimain 521
IRELAND
Dublin 1,024
ISRAEL
Tel Aviv 1,880
Jerusalem 562
ITALY
Rome 2,688
Milan 1,334
Naples 1,062
Turin 946
Palermo 695
Genoa 660
IVORY COAST
Abidjan 2,500
JAMAICA
Kingston 644
JAPAN
Tokyo-
Yokohama 26,836
Osaka 10,601
Nagoya 2,159
Sapporo 1,732
Kobe 1,509
Kyoto 1,452
Fukuoka 1,269
Kawasaki 1,200
Hiroshima 1,102
Kitakyushu 1,020
Sendai 951
Chiba 851
Sakai 806
Kumamoto 640
Okayama 605
Hamamatsu 561
Sagamihara 560
Funabashi 540
Kagoshima 540
Higashiosaka 515
JORDAN
Amman 1,300
Az-Zarqā 609
KAZAKSTAN
Almaty 1,151
Qaraghandy 613
KENYA
Nairobi 2,000
Mombasa 600
KOREA, NORTH
Pyŏngyang 2,639
Hamhŭng 775
Chŏngjin 754
Chinnampo 691
Sinŭiju 500
KOREA, SOUTH
Seoul 11,641
Pusan 3,814

Taegu 2,449
Inchon 2,308
Taejŏn 1,272
Kwangju 1,258
Ulsan 967
Sŏngnam 869
Puch'on 779
Suwŏn 756
Chŏnju 563
KYRGYZSTAN
Bishkek 584
LATVIA
Riga 840
LEBANON
Beirut 1,500
Tripoli 500
LIBYA
Tripoli 960
LITHUANIA
Vilnius 576
MACEDONIA
Skopje 541
MADAGASCAR
Antananarivo 1,053
MALAYSIA
Kuala Lumpur 1,145
MALI
Bamako 746
MAURITANIA
Nouakchott 600
MEXICO
Mexico City 15,643
Guadalajara 2,847
Monterrey 2,522
Puebla 1,055
León 872
Ciudad Juárez 798
Tijuana 743
Culiacán Rosales 602
Mexicali 602
Acapulco de
Juárez 592
Mérida 557
Chihuahua 530
San Luis Potosí 526
Aguascalientés 506
MOLDOVA
Chişinău 700
MONGOLIA
Ulan Bator 619
MOROCCO
Casablanca 2,943
Rabat-Salé 1,220
Marrakesh 602
Fès 564
MOZAMBIQUE
Maputo 2,000
NEPAL
Katmandu 535
NETHERLANDS
Amsterdam 1,100
Rotterdam 1,074
The Hague 695
Utrecht 546
NEW ZEALAND
Auckland 929
NICARAGUA
Managua 974
NIGERIA
Lagos 10,287
Ibadan 1,365
Ogbomosho 712
Kano 657
NORWAY
Oslo 714
PAKISTAN
Karachi 9,863
Lahore 5,085
Faisalabad 1,875
Peshawar 1,676
Gujranwala 1,663

Rawalpindi 1,290
Multan 1,257
Hyderabad 1,107
PARAGUAY
Asunción 945
PERU
Lima-Callao 6,601
Callao 638
Arequipa 620
Trujillo 509
PHILIPPINES
Manila 9,280
Quezon City 1,677
Davao 961
Cebu 688
Caloocan 643
POLAND
Warsaw 1,638
Lódz 826
Kraków 745
Wroclaw 643
Poznań 582
PORTUGAL
Lisbon 2,561
Oporto 1,174
ROMANIA
Bucharest 2,061
RUSSIA
Moscow 9,233
St Petersburg 4,883
Nizhniy
Novgorod 1,425
Novosibirsk 1,418
Yekaterinburg 1,347
Samara 1,223
Omsk 1,161
Chelyabinsk 1,125
Kazan 1,092
Ufa 1,092
Perm 1,086
Rostov 1,023
Volgograd 1,000
Krasnoyarsk 914
Voronezh 905
Saratov 899
Togliatti 689
Simbirsk 670
Izhevsk 653
Krasnodar 638
Vladivostok 637
Irkutsk 632
Yaroslavl 631
Khabarovsk 609
Barnaul 596
Novokuznetsk 593
Orenburg 558
Penza 551
Tyumen 550
Tula 535
Ryazan 526
Naberezhnyye-
Chelny 524
Kemerovo 513
Astrakhan 512
SAUDI ARABIA
Riyadh 2,000
Jedda 1,400
Mecca 618
Medina 500
SENEGAL
Dakar 1,729
SIERRA LEONE
Freetown 505
SINGAPORE
Singapore 2,874
SOMALIA
Mogadishu 1,000
SOUTH AFRICA
Cape Town 2,350
East Rand 1,379
Johannesburg 1,196

Durban 1,137
Pretoria 1,080
West Rand 870
Port Elizabeth 853
Vanderbijlpark-
Vereeniging 774
Soweto 597
Sasolburg 540
SPAIN
Madrid 3,041
Barcelona 1,631
Valencia 764
Sevilla 714
Zaragoza 607
Málaga 531
SRI LANKA
Colombo 1,863
SUDAN
Khartoum 561
Omdurman 526
SWEDEN
Stockholm 1,553
Göteborg 788
SWITZERLAND
Zürich 915
SYRIA
Damascus 2,230
Aleppo 1,640
Homs 644
TAIWAN
Taipei 2,653
Kaohsiung 1,405
Taichung 817
Tainan 700
Panchiao 544
TAJIKISTAN
Dushanbe 602
TANZANIA
Dar-es-Salaam 1,361
THAILAND
Bangkok 5,876
TOGO
Lomé 590
TUNISIA
Tunis 1,827
TURKEY
Istanbul 7,490
Ankara 3,028
Izmir 2,333
Adana 1,472
Bursa 1,317
Konya 1,040
Gaziantep 930
Icel 908
Antalya 734
Diyarbakir 677
Kocaeli 661
Urfa 649
Kayseri 648
Manisa 641
Hatay 561
Samsun 557
Eskisehir 508
Balikesir 501
UGANDA
Kampala 773
UKRAINE
Kiev 2,630
Kharkiv 1,555
Dnipropetrovsk 1,147
Donetsk 1,088
Odesa 1,046
Zaporizhzhya 887
Lviv 802
Kryvyy Rih 720
Mariupol 510
Mykolayiv 508
UNITED KINGDOM
London 8,089
Birmingham 2,373
Manchester 2,353

Liverpool 852
Glasgow 832
Leeds 529
Newcastle 525
UNITED STATES
New York 16,329
Los Angeles 12,410
Chicago 7,668
Philadelphia 4,949
Washington, DC 4,466
Detroit 4,307
Houston 3,653
Atlanta 3,331
Boston 3,240
Dallas 2,898
Minneapolis-
St Paul 2,688
San Diego 2,632
St Louis 2,536
Phoenix 2,473
Baltimore 2,458
Pittsburgh 2,402
Cleveland 2,222
San Francisco 2,182
Seattle 2,180
Tampa 2,157
Miami 2,025
Denver 1,796
Portland (Or.) 1,676
Kansas City (Mo.) 1,647
Cincinnati 1,581
San Jose 1,557
Norfolk 1,529
Indianapolis 1,462
Milwaukee 1,456
Sacramento 1,441
San Antonio 1,437
Columbus (Oh.) 1,423
New Orleans 1,309
Charlotte 1,260
Buffalo 1,189
Salt Lake City 1,178
Hartford 1,151
Oklahoma 1,007
Jacksonville 665
Omaha 663
Memphis 614
El Paso 579
Austin 514
Nashville 505
URUGUAY
Montevideo 1,326
UZBEKISTAN
Tashkent 2,106
VENEZUELA
Caracas 2,784
Maracaibo 1,364
Valencia 1,032
Maracay 800
Barquisimeto 745
Ciudad Guayana 524
VIETNAM
Ho Chi Minh
City 4,322
Hanoi 3,056
Haiphong 783
YEMEN
Sana 972
YUGOSLAVIA
Belgrade 1,137
ZAMBIA
Lusaka 982
ZIMBABWE
Harare 1,189
Bulawayo 622

* SAR = Special
Administrative Region
of China

GENERAL REFERENCE

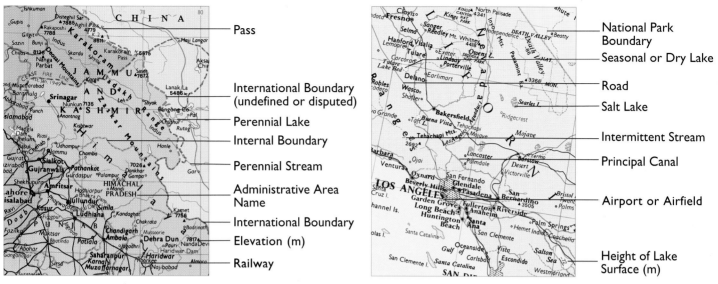

- Pass
- International Boundary (undefined or disputed)
- Perennial Lake
- Internal Boundary
- Perennial Stream
- Administrative Area Name
- International Boundary
- Elevation (m)
- Railway

- National Park Boundary
- Seasonal or Dry Lake
- Road
- Salt Lake
- Intermittent Stream
- Principal Canal
- Airport or Airfield
- Height of Lake Surface (m)

Settlements

Settlement symbols and type styles vary according to the scale of each map and indicate the importance of towns rather than specific population figures.

TIME ZONES

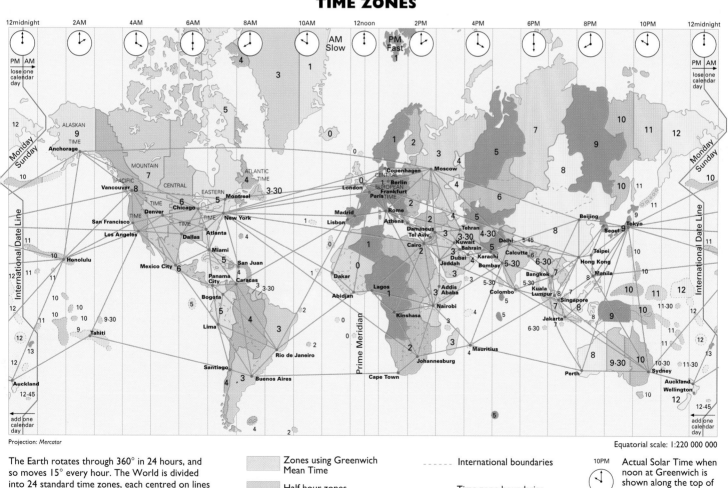

Projection: Mercator

Equatorial scale: 1:220 000 000

The Earth rotates through 360° in 24 hours, and so moves 15° every hour. The World is divided into 24 standard time zones, each centred on lines of longitude at 15° intervals.
The Greenwich meridian lies on the centre of the first zone. All places to the west of Greenwich are one hour behind for every 15° of longitude; places to the east are ahead by one hour for every 15°.

- Zones using Greenwich Mean Time
- Half hour zones
- Zones fast of Greenwich Mean Time
- Zones slow of Greenwich Mean Time

- - - - International boundaries
——— Time zone boundaries
——— International date line
——— Selected air routes

10PM Actual Solar Time when noon at Greenwich is shown along the top of the map.

Note: Certain of the time zones are affected by the incidence of "Summer Time" in countries where it is adopted.

CARTOGRAPHY BY PHILIP'S.

Projection: *Hammer Equal Area*

Hanoi ◉ Capital Cities

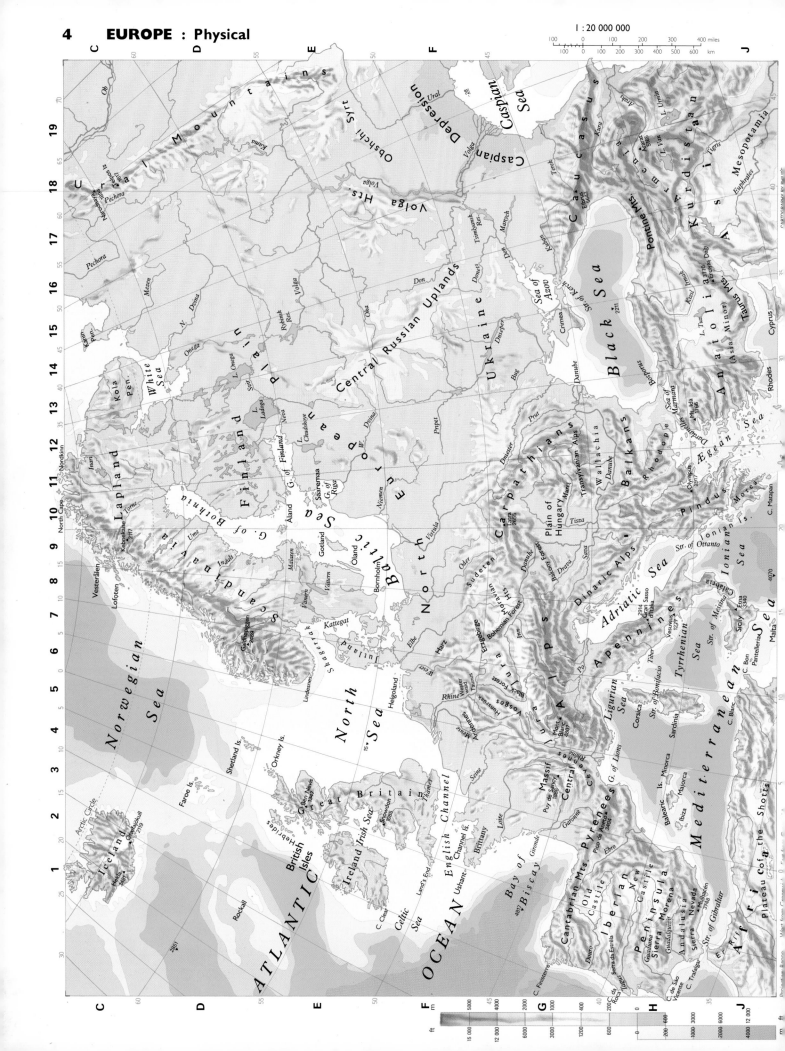

1 : 20 000 000

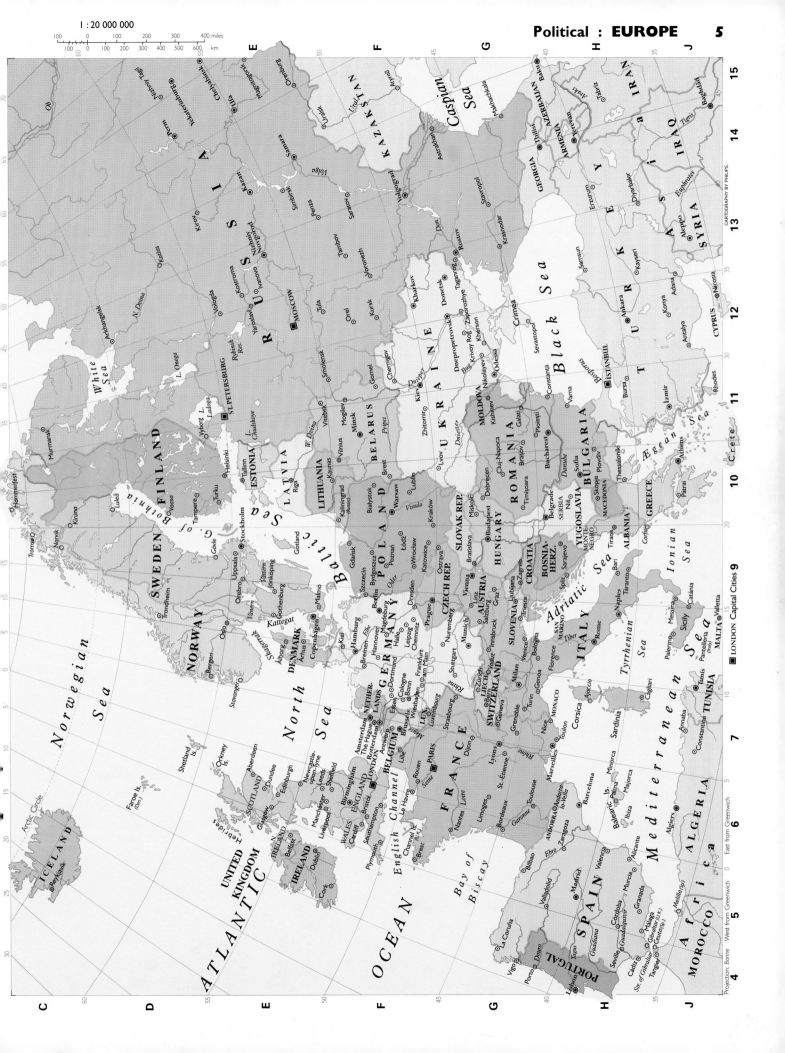

1 : 20 000 000

100   0   100   200   300   400 miles
100 50 0 100 200 300 400 500 600 km

E   F   45   G   40   H   35   J

15

14

13

CARTOGRAPHY BY PHILIPS

12

11

10   Crete

Projection: Bonne   West from Greenwich   0   East from Greenwich

■ LONDON Capital Cities 9

9

8

7

6

5

4

ARCTIC OCEAN labels and placenames:

Ob, Nizhny Tagil, Chelyabinsk, Yekaterinburg, Magnitogorsk, Orenburg

KAZAKSTAN

Caspian Sea

AZERBAIJAN Baku

ARMENIA Yerevan

GEORGIA Tbilisi

Makhachkala

I R A N Tabriz

Erzurum Diyarbakir

Aleppo SYRIA

Baghdad IRAQ

Tigris Euphrates

T U R K E Y

Ankara Kayseri Adana Konya Antalya

Samsun

CYPRUS Nicosia

Izmir Bursa ISTANBUL Bosporus

Rhodes

Æ g e a n S e a

GREECE Athens Patras Thessaloniki

Ionian Sea

ALBANIA Tirana Corfu

MACEDONIA Skopje

MONTE NEGRO SERBIA Niš Belgrade

BULGARIA Sofia Plovdiv Varna

ROMANIA Bucharest Galati Cluj-Napoca Braşov Timişoara

Danube

MOLDOVA Kishinev

Dniester Odessa Nikolayev Kherson Krivoy Rog Zaporozhye

U K R A I N E Kiev Lvov Zhitomir Dnepropetrovsk Donetsk Taganrog

Dnieper Bug Pripet

Kharkov Rostov Krasnodar Stavropol Volgograd

Black Sea

Sevastopol Crimea Constanta

Don

R U S S I A

MOSCOW St.PETERSBURG

Smolensk Orel Kursk Voronezh Tula Penza Tambov Saratov Samara

Vitebsk Mogilev Gomel Chernigov

Nizhny Novgorod Ivanovo Kostroma Yaroslavl Vologda Kazan

Rybinsk Res. Volga Ulyanovsk Simbirsk

L. Onega N. Dvina Arkhangelsk

White Sea Murmansk

BELARUS Minsk Brest

Pripet

L. Ladoga L. Chudskoye Vyborg Helsinki

ESTONIA Tallinn

LATVIA Riga W. Dvina

LITHUANIA Vilnius Kaunas

Kaliningrad (Russia)

FINLAND Tampere Turku Vaasa

Bothnia, G. of

SWEDEN Stockholm Uppsala Örebro Gävle Vänern Vättern Jönköping Gothenburg

Luleå Kiruna Narvik

Hammerfest Tromsø

NORWAY Oslo Bergen Trondheim Stavanger Kristiansand Skagerrak

Norwegian Sea

Baltic Sea Gotland Öland

POLAND Warsaw Gdańsk Szczecin Bydgoszcz Poznań Łódź Wrocław Katowice Kraków Lublin Białystok

Vistula Oder

DENMARK Copenhagen Århus Ålborg Odense Kattegat

Kiel Hamburg Bremen Hannover Berlin Magdeburg Halle Leipzig Dresden Chemnitz

G E R M A N Y Cologne Bonn Frankfurt am Main Wiesbaden Stuttgart Nuremberg Munich Dortmund Essen Düsseldorf

Elbe Rhine

CZECH REP. Prague

SLOVAK REP. Bratislava

AUSTRIA Vienna Linz Salzburg Innsbruck Graz

HUNGARY Budapest Miskolc Debrecen

SLOVENIA Ljubljana

CROATIA Zagreb

BOSNIA-HERZ. Sarajevo Split

YUGOSLAVIA

Adriatic Sea

SWITZERLAND Zürich Geneva Bern Basle

LIECH. Vaduz

ITALY Rome Milan Turin Genoa Venice Bologna Florence Naples Bari Taranto Palermo Messina Catania

SAN MARINO Tiber

MONACO Nice Corsica Ajaccio Sardinia Cagliari

Tyrrhenian Sea

Sicily MALTA Valletta Pantelleria (Italy)

NETHER-LANDS Amsterdam The Hague Rotterdam

BELGIUM Brussels Antwerp Meuse

LUX. Luxembourg

F R A N C E PARIS Lyons Marseilles Toulouse Bordeaux Nantes Strasbourg Dijon Rouen Le Havre St-Étienne Grenoble Toulon Limoges

Seine Loire Rhône Garonne

English Channel Channel Is. Brest

UNITED KINGDOM LONDON ENGLAND Birmingham Manchester Liverpool Leeds Sheffield Newcastle-upon-Tyne Bristol Southampton Plymouth Cardiff WALES

SCOTLAND Edinburgh Glasgow Aberdeen Dundee

Shetland Is. Orkney Is. Hebrides

IRELAND Dublin Belfast Cork

North Sea

A T L A N T I C O C E A N

ICELAND Reykjavik

Faroe Is. (Den.)

Arctic Circle

Bay of Biscay

ANDORRA Andorra-la-Vella

S P A I N Madrid Barcelona Valencia Zaragoza Bilbao Valladolid Córdoba Seville Málaga Granada Murcia Alicante La Coruña Vigo

Balearic Is. Palma Majorca Minorca Ibiza

Ebro Guadiana Guadalquivir Tagus

PORTUGAL Lisbon Porto

Str. of Gibraltar Gibraltar (U.K.) Ceuta (Sp.)

M e d i t e r r a n e a n S e a

MOROCCO Tangier Melilla A f r i c a

ALGERIA Algiers Oran Constantine Annaba

TUNISIA Tunis

1 : 10 000 000

100 50 0 50 100 150 200 miles
100 0 100 200 300 km

1   2   3   4   5   6   7   10   11   12   13   16

ICELAND
On the same scale West from Greenwich

A
Ísafjörður   Siglufjörður
Húnaflói   Sauðárkrókur   Húsavik
Breiðafjörður   Akureyri
B   Seyðisfjörður

Akranes
Reykjavik   Vatnajökull
Keflavik   2119 ▲
C

8   9

ARCTIC OCEAN
North Cape
Nordkinn
Hammerfest   Vardø
Søroya   Vadsø   Varanger Fd
Kirkenes   Pechenga
Senja   Tromsø   **Murmansk**
Vesterålen   Inari   L. Inari
Kebnekaise   Kiruna   Porttipahta   Lokka Res.   Kola Peninsula
2123   Res.   Kirovsk
Narvik   L. Torne   Torne
Storlulea   Kandalaksha
Bodø   Sulitjelma   Gällivare   Arctic Circle   White Sea
1913   Rovaniemi
Hornavan   Kemi   Belomorsk   **Arkhangelsk**
Storavan   Boden   Kemi   Onega
Vega   Storuman   Luleå   Tornio   L. Kem   Onega
Vilhelmina   Piteå   Haparanda   Oulu
Vikna   Skellefte   Skellefteå   Raahe   Oulu   Karelia
Folda Fjord   Ume   L. Oulu   Kajaani   L. Onega
Trondheim Fjord   Åsele   Vännäs   Umeå   Iisalmi   Petrozavodsk
Kristiansund   Östersund   Örnsköldsvik   **FINLAND**
Molde   Trondheim   Vaasa   Kuopio
Ålesund   Storsjön   Bräcke   Härnösand   Joensuu   L. Onega
Stadlandet   Dovre Fjell   Ange   Jyväskylä   Saimaa
Snøhetta   Ljusnan   Sundsvall   Tampere   Imatra
Florø   2286   Galdhøpiggen   Hudiksvall   Pori   Hämeenlinna   Vyborg   St. Petersburg   Cherepovets
Høyanger   2469   Söderhamn   Lahti   (Leningrad)   Tikhvin
Sogne Fjord   Lillehammer   Mora   Turku   **Helsinki**   Kronstadt
Bergen   Gävle   Uusikaupunki   Hanko   Kotka   Malaya Vishera
Hardanger Fjord   Dannemora   Åland Is.   Gulf of Finland   Borovichi   Rybinsk Reservoir
Haugesund   Mjøsa   Sala   Västerås   Uppsala   Tallinn   Narva   Novgorod   Vyshniy Volochek
Oslo   Hjälmaren   Hiiumaa   Kohtla-Järve   L. Ilmen
Drammen   Karlstad   Eskilstuna   **ESTONIA**   Luga   Staraya Russa
Stavanger   Skien   Fredrikstad   Örebro   **Stockholm**   Saaremaa   Pärnu   Tartu   Pskov
Arendal   Larvik   Halden   Vänern   Norrköping   Västervik   Visby   L. Chudskoye   **RUSSIA**   Vyshniy Volochek
Egersund   Oslo Fd   Vättern   Linköping   Gotland   Valga   Kholm   Valdai Hills   Tver
Kristiansand   Mandal   Trollhättan   Jönköping   Gulf of Riga   Pskov   Volga   MOSCOW
Lindesnes   Skagen (The Skaw)   Borås   **LATVIA**   Velikiye Luki   Rzhev
Skagerrak   Gothenburg   Göta   **Riga**   Jelgava   Nevel
Lim Fjord   Ålborg   Varberg   Oskarshamn   Öland   Ventspils   Daugavpils
Jutland   Kattegat   Halmstad   Kalmar   Liepaja   Daugava   Vitebsk
Aarhus   Randers   The Sound   Karlskrona   Klaipeda   **LITHUANIA**   Smolensk   Kaluga
DENMARK   Helsingborg   Bornholm   Sovetsk   **Kaunas**   **Vilnius**   Mogilev
Esbjerg   **Copenhagen**   Lund   (RUSSIA)   **Kaliningrad**   Minsk   Bryansk
Odense   Fyn   **Malmö**   Gdynia   **BELARUS**
Flensburg   Sjælland   Gdańsk   Suwalki   Slutsk   Bobruysk   Gomel
Helgoland   Gedser   Sassnitz   Elblag   Olsztyn   Grodno   Baranovichi   Pinsk   Pripet
Kiel   Stralsund   Rügen   Szczecin   Toruń   Białystok   Chernigov
Lübeck   Rostock   Bydgoszcz   Poznań   Plock   **Warsaw**   Brest   Konotop
Hamburg   Vistula   Lutsk   Rovno   Zhitomir   **Kiev**
Bremen   Elbe   **BERLIN**   Frankfurt   **POLAND**   Łódź   Radom   Lublin
Hannover   Braunschweig   Magdeburg   Oder   Wrocław   Kielce   UKRAINE   Poltava
Münster   Weser   Halle   Legnica   Częstochowa   Przemyśl   Lvov
Dortmund   Harz   Leipzig   Gorlitz   Katowice   **Kraków**
Kassel   Erfurt   Chemnitz   **Dresden**
Wiesbaden   Plauen   Plzeň   Prague   CZECH REP.
Frankfurt   Würzburg   Nuremberg   Heidelberg

ATLANTIC OCEAN
Arctic Circle

N O R W A Y
S W E D E N
G E R M A N Y

Norrland
Svealand
Götaland

Gulf of Bothnia
BALTIC SEA

Projection: Conical with two standard parallels   East from Greenwich   COPYRIGHT. GEORGE PHILIP & SON LTD.

9   10   11   12   13   14

1 : 5 000 000

50   0   50   100 miles
50   0   50   100   150 km

CARTOGRAPHY BY PHILIP'S.

Corsica
C. Corse
Bastia
Calvi
Mte. Cinto 2710   Corte
Mte. Rotondo 2625
2136
Ajaccio
Porto-Vecchio
Bonifacio

GERMANY

AUSTRIA

SWITZERLAND

ITALY

BELGIUM

LUXEMBOURG

UNITED KINGDOM

SPAIN

ANDORRA

F R A N C E

PARIS

MARSEILLES

LYONS

MEDITERRANEAN SEA

Bay of Biscay

English Channel

Golfe de Gascogne

Golfe du Lion

East from Greenwich

West from Greenwich

Projection: conical with two standard parallels

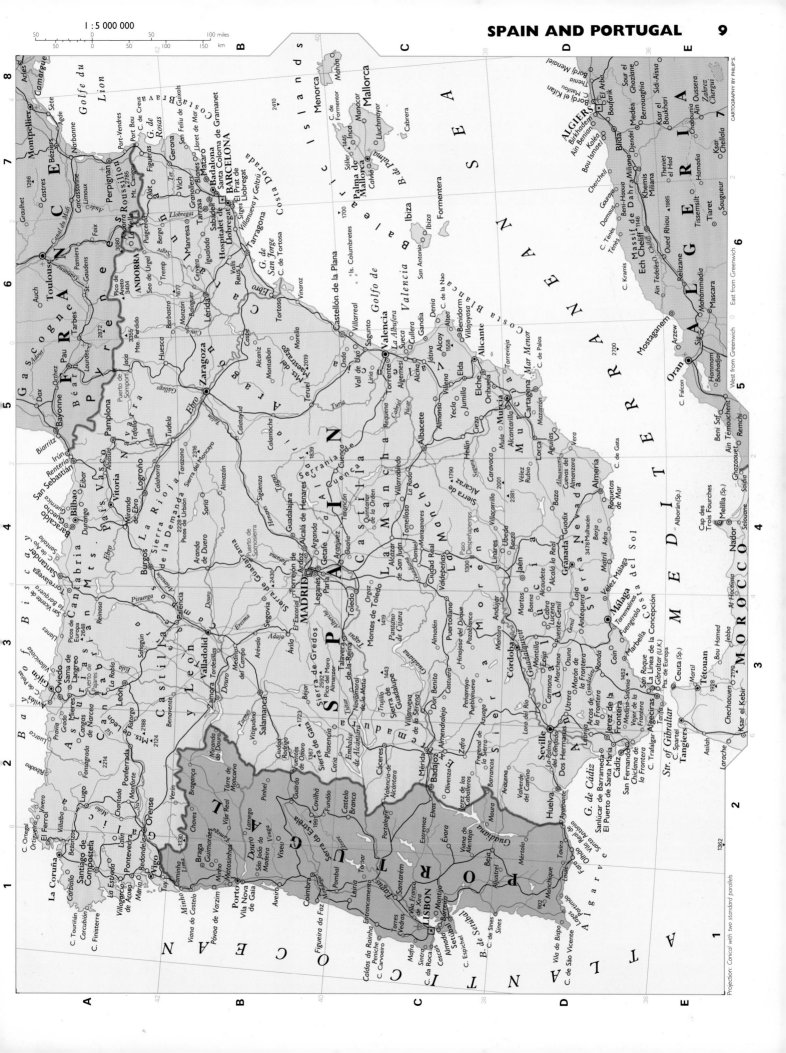

1 : 5 000 000

Projection: Conical with two standard parallels

CARTOGRAPHY BY PHILIP'S

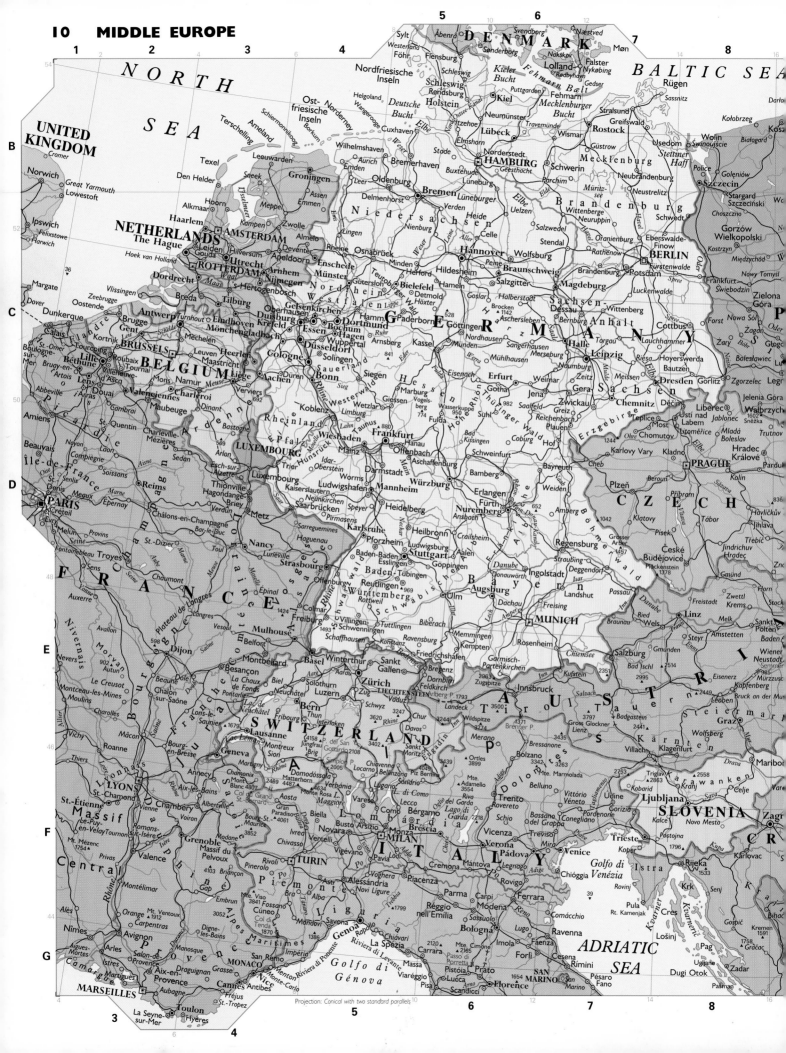

A   B   C   D

12 11 10 9 8 7 6 5 4 3 2 1

Khalmer Yu 1363
Vorkuta
Labytnangi
Salekhard
Berezovo
Sosva
Ivdel
Kalya
Krasnoturinsk
Serov
Nizhniy Tagil
Sverdlovsk
YEKATERINBURG
Pervouralsk
Miass
Zlatoust
Yaman Tau 1640
Beloretsk
Magnitogorsk
S
Orsk
Novotroitsk
Orenburg
Kumertau

Telpos Iz 1617
Narodnaya 1894
Inta
Usa
Ust Usa
Arctic Circle
Troitsko-Pechorsk
U   r   a   l
U   r
M   O
U
n   s
Kungur
Kizel
Berezniki
Solikamsk 1569
Chusovoy
Lysva
PERM
Kama
Cherdyn
Votkinsk
Belaya
UFA
BASHKORTOSTAN
Birsk
Sterlitamak
Salavat
Sorochinsk
Buzuluk

Bolshezemelsk
Tundra
Naryan-Mar
Pechora
Ukhta
Sosnogorsk
Zheleznodorozhny
Syktyvkar
Nyazepetrovsk
337
Glazov
Izhevsk
UDMURTIA
A
Sarapul
Naberezhnyye Chelny
Dimitrovgrod
TATARSTAN
Buguruslan
Bugulma

G. of Pechora
Ust Tsilma
Pechora
Koslan
463
Mkun
Vychegda
Murashi
Slobodskoy
Nolinsk
Kirov
Vyatka
Yoshkar Ola
MARI EL
Cheboksary
KAZAN
CHUVASHIA
Alaty
SAMARA
Togliatti
Reservoir
Novokuybyshevsk
Syzran
351
Kuznetsk
Volsk
Balakovo
H

Kolguyev
Kanin Pen.
Chesha B.
Mezen
Mezen
Karpogory
Pinega
Velikiy Ustyug
Totma
Kotelnich
Sharya
Shakhunya
Vetluga
Volga
Simbirsk
Saransk
MORDVINIA
Penza
Serdobsk

C. Kanin Nos
Dvina
Dvina Sea
Arkhangelsk
Plesetsk
Nyandoma
Velsk
Konosha
Kharovsk
Vologda
Bui
Kostroma
Kineshma
Ivanovo
Gorki Reservoir
Nizhniy Novgorod
Dzerzhinsk
Arzamas
Murom
Morshansk
Tambov

Severodvinsk
Onega
Onega
G. of Onega
Beloye L.
Belozersk
Cherepovets
Rybinsk Reservoir
Yaroslavl
Rostov
Vladimir
Orekhovo-Zuyevo
Ryazan
Michurinsk
Lipetsk
Yelets

Rybachi Pen.
Kola B.
Murmansk
1191
Monchegorsk
Imandra L.
Kola Pen.
White Sea
Kandalaksha G.
Kem
Top L.
Belomorsk
Povenets
Kondopoga L.
Onega
Podporozhye
Lodeynoye Pole
Novaya Ladoga
L. Ilmen
Borovichi
Vyshniy Volochek
343
Tver
Sergiyev Posad
Moscow
Podolsk
Serpukhov
Kaluga
293
Tula
Novomoskovsk
Orel
Bryansk

Pechenga
Kandalaksha
Pya L.
Kuito Ls.
417 L. Seg
Medvezhyegorsk
Petrozavodsk
KARELIA
Olonets
Svir
L. Ladoga
Priozersk
Volkhov
Staraya Russa
Velikiye Luki
Rzhev
Vyazma
Smolensk
Roslavl

L. Inari
NORWAY
Lapland
Muonio
Torne
Kiruna
Torne L.
2117
Kebnekaise
Gällivare
SWEDEN
Kalix
Luleå
Oulu
Kemi
Kemijärvi
Rovaniemi
Sodankylä
Kuopio
FINLAND
Lahti
Tampere
Turku
HELSINKI
Pori
Åland Is. (Ahvenanmaa)
STOCKHOLM
Hiiumaa
Saaremaa
Tallinn
Pärnu
ESTONIA
Tartu
Chudskoye L.
Pskov
Velikaya
Pskov
LATVIA
RIGA
Jelgava
Daugava
LITHUANIA
Siauliai
Vilnius
Kaunas
Klaipeda
Liepaja
Ventspils
G. of Riga
Minsk
BELARUS
Baranovichi
Bobruysk
Mogilev
Vitebsk
Orsha
Dnieper
Pripet Marshes
Pinsk
Gomel
Chernigov
Desna

Narvik
Mo
Bodo
1916
Kiruna
Ume
Umeå
Angerman
Sundsvall
Söderhamn
Gulf of Bothnia
Hanko
G. of Finland
ST. PETERSBURG (Leningrad)
Neva
Narva
Luga
Novgorod
L. Ilmen
Volkhov
Dvina
Daugavpils
346
228
Grodno
Bialystok
Brest
Bug
Lomza
WARSAW
POLAND
Lublin
(RUSSIA)
Kaliningrad
Sovetsk
Neman
65 60 55 50 45 40 30 25 20 15

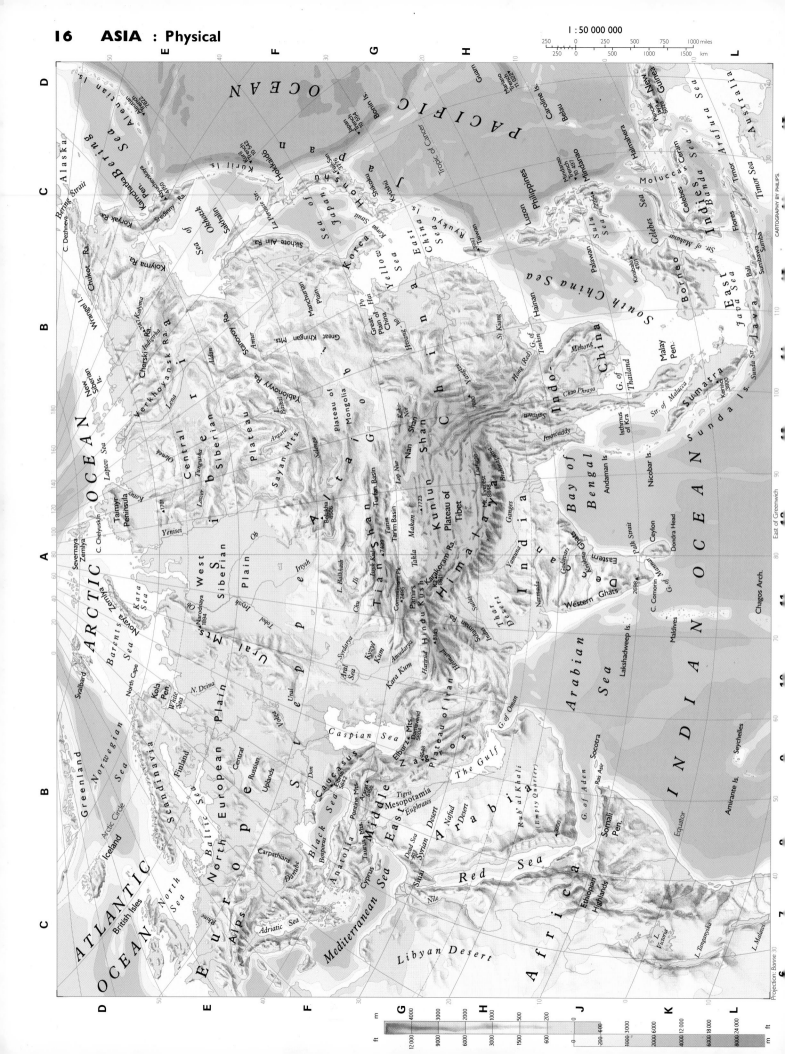

1 : 50 000 000

CARTOGRAPHY BY PHILIPS

Projection: Bonne

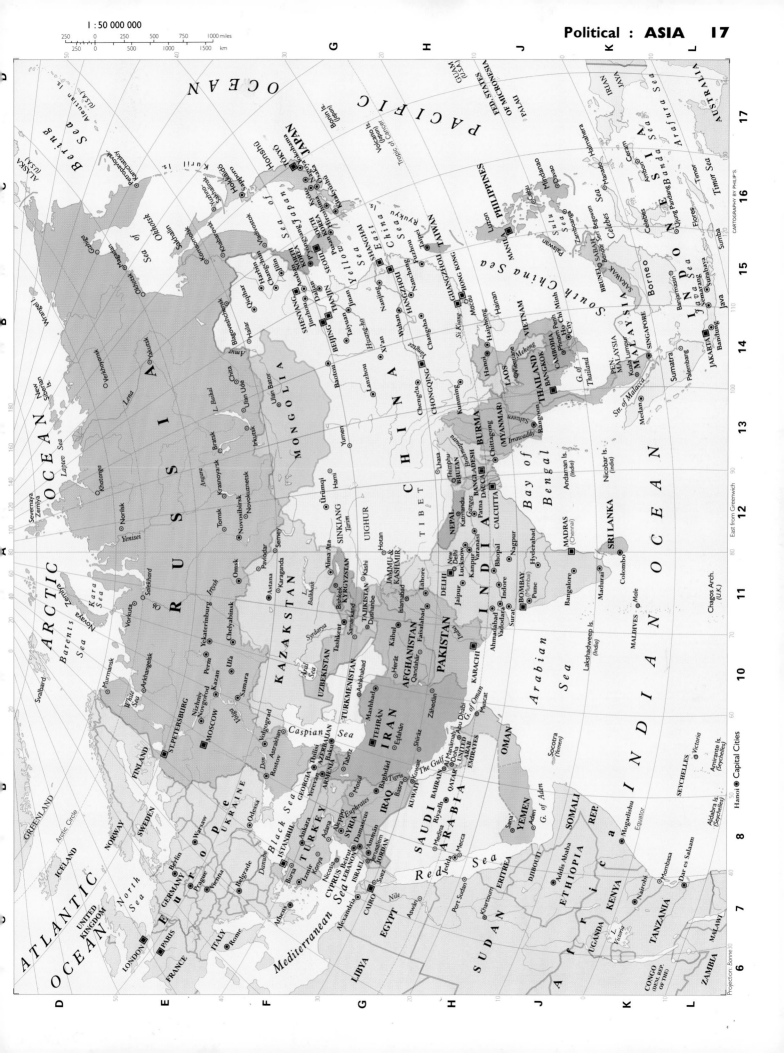

1 : 50 000 000

250   0   250   500   750   1000 miles
50 0   40
250   0   500   1000   1500   km

1 : 35 000 000

200   0   200   400   600   800 miles
400   0   400   800   1200 km

Projection: Lambert's Conical Orthomorphic

East from Greenwich

Seas and Oceans

Bering Sea · Gulf of Anadyr · Sea of Okhotsk · East Siberian Sea · Laptev Sea · Kara Sea · Barents Sea · Norwegian Sea · North Sea · Baltic Sea · White Sea · Gulf of Bothnia · Gulf of Finland · Black Sea · Sea of Azov · Caspian Sea · Aral Sea · L. Balkhash · Yellow Sea · East China Sea · Sea of Japan · Gulf of Oman · The Gulf

Regions / Ranges

Chukot Ra. · Kolyma Ra. · Sredinny Ra. · Kamchatka · Sikhote Alin Ra. · Cherski Ra. · Verkhoyansk Ra. · Stanovoy Ra. · Dzhugdzhur Ra. · Yablonovyy Ra. · Central Siberian Plateau · West Siberian Plain · Ural Mountains · Taimyr Peninsula · Severnaya Zemlya · Novaya Zemlya · Franz Josef Land · New Siberian Is. · Wrangel I. · Svalbard (Spitsbergen) · Great Khingan Mts. · Tarbagatai Ra. · Ala Shan · Nan Shan · Kunlun Shan · Tien Shan · Himalaya · Hindu Kush · Elburz Mts. · Zagros Mts. · Caucasus · Takla Makan · Kyzyl Kum · Kara Kum · Ustyurt Plateau · Dzungaria

Countries

RUSSIA · KAZAKSTAN · UZBEKISTAN · TURKMENISTAN · KYRGYZSTAN · TAJIKISTAN · MONGOLIA · CHINA · SINKIANG-UIGHUR · TIBET · INDIA · PAKISTAN · AFGHANISTAN · IRAN · TURKEY · GEORGIA · ARMENIA · AZERBAIJAN · KOREA · JAPAN · TAIWAN · UNITED KINGDOM · DENMARK · GERMANY · POLAND · ROMANIA · MOLDOVA · UKRAINE · BELARUS · LITHUANIA · LATVIA · ESTONIA · FINLAND · NORWAY · SWEDEN · OMAN · UNITED ARAB EMIRATES · QATAR · BAHRAIN · KUWAIT

Cities

Moscow · St. Petersburg · Murmansk · Arkhangelsk · Vologda · Yaroslavl · Ivanovo · Nizhniy Novgorod · Kazan · Samara · Orenburg · Ufa · Perm · Izhevsk · Kirov · Yekaterinburg · Chelyabinsk · Magnitogorsk · Nizhniy Tagil · Serov · Tyumen · Kurgan · Omsk · Novosibirsk · Tomsk · Kemerovo · Prokopyevsk · Novokuznetsk · Leninsk Kuznetskiy · Barnaul · Biysk · Pavlodar · Semey · Krasnoyarsk · Irkutsk · Ulan Ude · Chita · Bratsk · Ust Ilimsk · Tula · Orel · Kursk · Voronezh · Lipetsk · Tambov · Penza · Saratov · Volgograd · Astrakhan · Rostov · Krasnodar · Stavropol · Grozny · Makhachkala · Vladikavkaz · Baku · Tbilisi · Yerevan · Tabriz · Tehran · Mashhad · Esfahan · Yazd · Kerman · Shiraz · Ahvaz · Abadan · Baghdad · Basra · Mosul · Erzurum · Ararat · Vladivostok · Khabarovsk · Komsomolsk · Blagoveshchensk · Yuzhno-Sakhalinsk · Magadan · Petropavlovsk-Kamchatskiy · Anadyr · Noril'sk · Dudinka · Vorkuta · Kotlas · Petrozavodsk · Syktyvkar · Kaliningrad · Vilnius · Kaunas · Riga · Tallinn · Minsk · Gomel · Smolensk · Tver · Rybinsk · Kiev · Kharkov · Zhitomir · Lvov · Krivoy Rog · Dnepropetrovsk · Zaporozhye · Donetsk · Mariupol · Nikolayev · Kherson · Odessa · Sevastopol · Kerch · Novorossiysk · Taganrog · Helsinki · Tampere · Oslo · Bergen · Trondheim · Stockholm · Copenhagen · Hamburg · Berlin · Szczecin · Warsaw · Katowice · Edinburgh · Karaganda · Astana · Kokshetau · Kostanay · Aktobe · Atyrau · Aralsk · Kzyl Orda · Almaty (Alma Ata) · Bishkek · Tashkent · Samarkand · Bukhara · Dushanbe · Khujand · Ashkhabad · Mary · Chardzhou · Nukus · Herat · Qondoz · Kabul · Qandahar · Quetta · Peshawar · Islamabad · Rawalpindi · Lahore · Faisalabad · Multan · Amritsar · Ludhiana · Delhi · Meerut · Srinagar · Urumqi · Kashgar · Yining · Turpan · Ulan Bator · Harbin · Changchun · Shenyang · Dalian · Beijing · Tianjin · Jinan · Qingdao · Zhengzhou · Xi'an · Lanzhou · Xining · Chengdu · Chongqing · Wuhan · Changsha · Nanchang · Nanjing · Shanghai · Hangzhou · Fuzhou · Xiamen · Guangzhou · Taipei · Seoul · Pusan · Pyongyang · Tōkyō · Yokohama · Kyōto · Ōsaka · Kōbe · Nagoya · Sapporo · Niigata · Sendai

Islands

Sakhalin · Hokkaido · Honshu · Shikoku · Kyushu · Kuril Is. · Ryukyu Islands · Komandorskiye · Hainan · Kolguyev I. · Vaygach I. · Komsomolets I. · October Revolution I. · Bolshevik I. · St. Lawrence I. (US)

Rivers

Ob · Irtysh · Yenisey · Lena · Aldan · Vilyuy · Angara · Amur · Kolyma · Indigirka · Yana · Olenek · Khatanga · Lower Tunguska · Volga · Don · Dnieper · Ural · Syrdarya · Amudarya · Hwang-ho · Yangtze · Mekong · Tigris · Euphrates · N. Dvina · Pechora · Kama · Oka · Desna

Arctic Circle · Tropic of Cancer · International dateline · North Cape

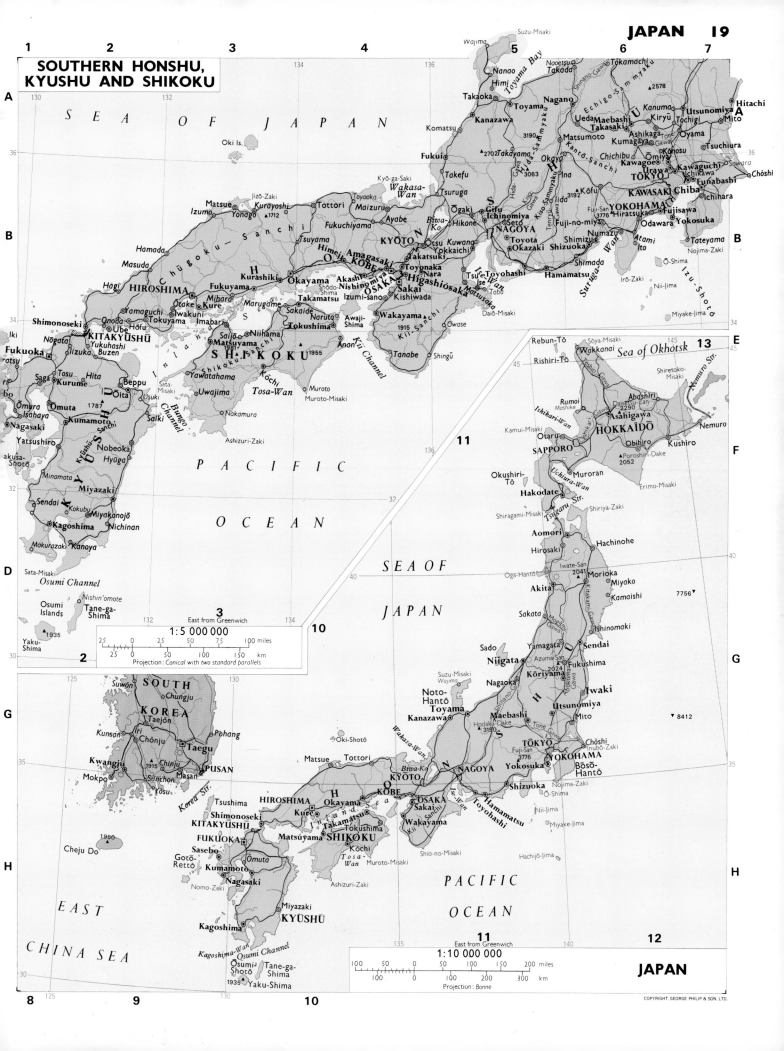

1 2 3 4 5

50

KAZAKSTAN

Karsakpay
Karaganda
Karkaralinsk
1565
Semey
Oskemen
Rubtsovsk
Belukha 4506
Zyryanovsk

RUSSIA
Western Sayan
Tannu Ola
Munku Sardyk 3491
Khuaem
Angarsk Cheremkhovo
Irkutsk
455

Ayaguz
Tarbagatai Ra.
Lake Zaisan
Altay
Fuyun
Uvs Nuur
Ulaangom
Har Us Nuur
Hovd
Döröö Nuur
Ulyosutay
Hyargas Nuur
Khangai
Hatgal
Hövsgöl Nuur
Tsetserleg
Selenge Mörön
Orhon Gol
Ulan Bat
Dzuun

B

342
Lake Balkhash
Taldy-Kurgan
Chu
Ala Tau
Ala Kul
Dzungarian Gates
Tacheng
Karamay
Fuhai
Ulungur
Altai
MONGO
4362
Buyanhongor
Dalandzadgad

Bishkek (Frunze)
Dzhambul
Issyk-Kul
Alma Ata
Yining
Ili
Bole
Usu
Dzungaria
Shan
Qitai
G

Namangan
Andizhan
KYRGYZSTAN
1609
Pik Pobedy 7439
Naryn
Ürümqi
5445
Turpan -154
Hami
4925
Gaxun Nur

Kashi
Aksu
Kuqa
Korla
UIGHUR
Bosten (Bagrax) Hu
Kuruktag

40

SINKIANG
Tarim He
Tarim Basin
Lop Nor
Anxi
Dunhuang
Yumen
Jiayuguan
Ala Shan
Wuhai 2
Alxa Zuoqi
NINGXIA
Yincuan
HUIZU
Wuzh

Shache
Yecheng
Takla Makan
1635
Hotan
Yutian
Qiemo
Ruoqiang
Altun Shan
Nan Shan
6346
Zhangye
Zhongwe
Wuwei

Karakoram
K2 8611
8126
JAMMU & KASHMIR
Srinagar
Leh
Karakoram Pass 5575
Kunlun
7723
Da Qaidam
Qaidam Pendi
Golmud
Tianjun
Qinghai Hu 3205
Dulan
Gonghe
Xining
Lanzhou
Pingliang
ZIZHIQU

C

Rutog
Shan
Ngoring Hu 4237
Gyaring Hu
Maqen
Linxia
Tianshui
Baoji

Gar
TIBET
Tanglha Range
Amdo
Yüshu
Bayan Har Shan
6094
Huang-ho
Wudu
4113
Min Xian
Hanzhong
Fialing

Nanda Devi 7817
Burang
Mapam Yumco
Siling Co 4495
Nagqu
Mekong
Garze
Daxue Shan
Mianyang
Daxian
S

30

Dehra Dun
Zhongba
Xainza
Nam Co 4627
Qamdo
Yangtze (Jinsha)
Yalong
Gogga Shan 7600
CHENGDU
U
Hanzhong

Meerut
Moradabad
Bareilly
HIMALAYA
8221 Dhaulagiri
NEPAL
Nyenchen Tanglha Range
Lhasa
Namcha Barwa 7756
Bomi
Zhongdian
Wutongqiao
Neijiang
Nanchong
Hechua

DELHI
Aligarh
Agra
Ghaghra
Lhazê
Xigaze
Yarlung Zangbo
Yamzho Yumco
Zayü
5881
Xichang
Dailang Shan
Luzhou
Yibin
Zigong
CHO (Chun)

KANPUR
Gwalior
LUCKNOW
Katmandu
Gorakhpur
Everest 8848
Thimphu
BHUTAN
Dibrugarh
Zhaotong
Zunyi
Wu

D

Jhansi
Allahabad
Ganga
Patna
Kôch Bihar
Brahmaputra
Tezpur
Packai Hills
3411
Lijiang
Dongchuan
Zhanyi
GUIZH

INDIA
Varanasi
Gauhati
Khasi Hills
Imphal 3824
Myitkyina
Xiaguan
Guiya
Anshun
D

Tropic of Cancer
Rajshahi
BANGLADESH
Silchar
Bhamo
Baoshan
KUNMING
Xingyi
Hechi
GU

Jabalpur
Ranchi
Asansol
DACCA (Dhaka)
Narayanganj
Luxi
YUNNAN
Gejiu
Wenshan
Hongshui
Bose
ZHU

Jamshedpur
Haora
Khulna
CALCUTTA
CHITTAGONG
BURMA (M
Myitkyina
3143 (Black)
Pingxiang
Qinz

NAGPUR
Raipur
Indravati
Mahanadi
Arakan Yoma
Victoria 3053
Mandalay
2650
Song Da (Black)
Nanning
VIETNAM

20

Cuttack
BAY OF
Akyab
Irrawaddy
Y
Pegu Yoma
HANOI
Hoa-Binh
HAIPHONG Gulf

E

Warangal
Vishakhapatnam
BENGAL
Yamethin
2463 THAILAND
Salween
Mekong
Luang Prabang
LAOS
Toungoo
Tonki

80

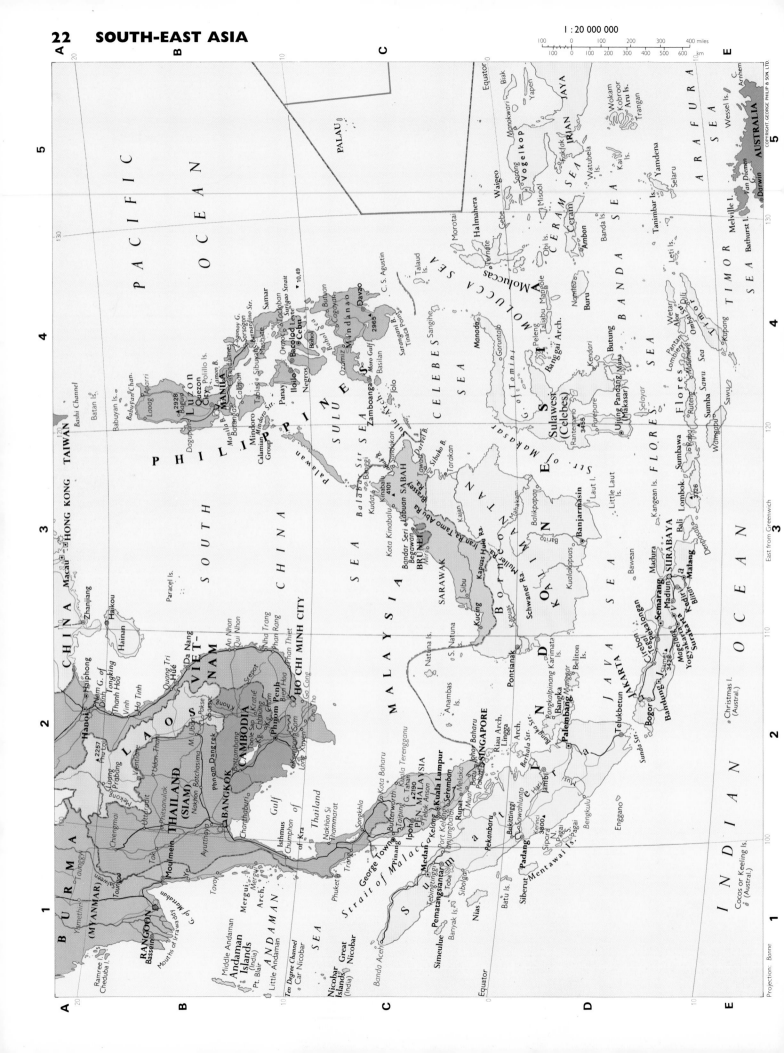

1 : 10 000 000

100   50   0   100   150   200 miles
100   0   100   200   300 km

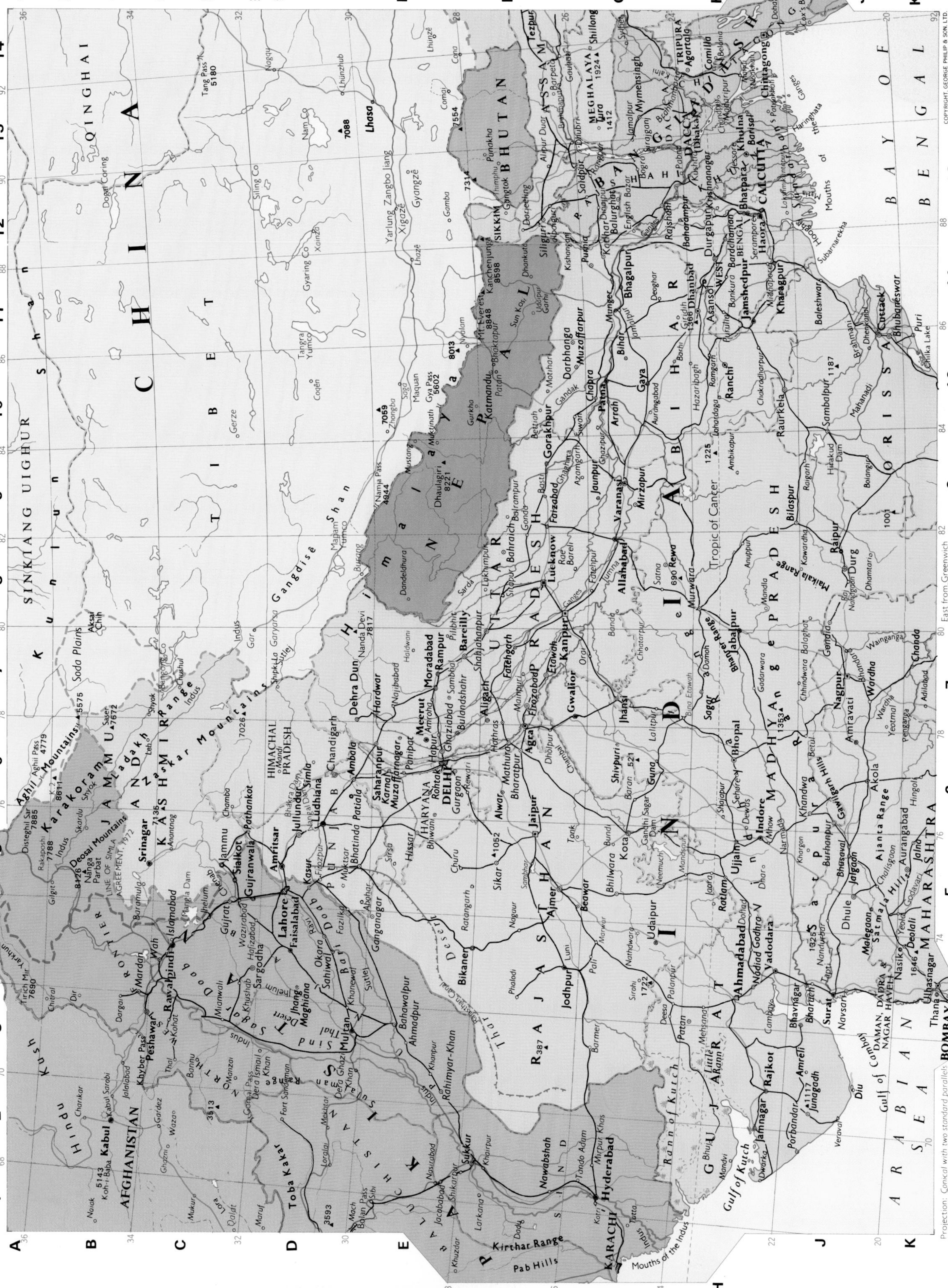

Projection: Conical with two standard parallels

East from Greenwich

QINGHAI

C H I N A

SINKIANG UIGHUR

Kun lun Shan

T I B E T

Lhasa
7088

Soda Plains
Aksai Chin

AFGHANISTAN
Kabul
Hindu Kush
Khyber Pass
Peshawar

Karakoram Range
Nanga Parbat
JAMMU AND KASHMIR
LINE OF CONTROL
SIMLA AGREEMENT, 1972
Srinagar
Jammu

HIMACHAL PRADESH
Chandigarh
Simla
Dehra Dun

PUNJAB
Amritsar
Lahore
Faisalabad
Ludhiana

H i m a l a y a

Kathmandu
N E P A L
Mt. Everest 8848
Kanchenjunga 8598
SIKKIM
BHUTAN
Gangtok
Thimphu

ASSAM
MEGHALAYA
Shillong

B A N G L A D E S H
DACCA (Dhaka)

TRIPURA
Agartala
Chittagong
Cox's Bazar

HARYANA
DELHI
Gurgaon

U T T A R P R A D E S H
Meerut
Moradabad
Bareilly
Lucknow
Kanpur
Allahabad
Varanasi

Gorakhpur

B I H A R
Patna
Gaya
Ranchi
Dhanbad

WEST BENGAL
CALCUTTA
Haora
Kharagpur
Asansol

R A J A S T H A N
Jaipur
Jodhpur
Bikaner
Ajmer
Kota
Udaipur

Thar Desert

M A D H Y A P R A D E S H
Bhopal
Indore
Jabalpur
Gwalior
Raipur
Nagpur

Tropic of Cancer

O R I S S A
Cuttack
Bhubaneswar
Puri

PAKISTAN
Islamabad
Rawalpindi
Gujranwala
Sialkot
Multan
Bahawalpur

B A L U C H I S T A N
Kirthar Range

S I N D
KARACHI
Hyderabad
Sukkur
Mouths of the Indus

Rann of Kutch
Gulf of Kutch

G U J A R A T
Ahmadabad
Vadodara
Surat
Rajkot
Bhavnagar
Jamnagar

M A H A R A S H T R A
BOMBAY
Nasik
Aurangabad

A R A B I A N S E A

B A Y O F B E N G A L

East from Greenwich

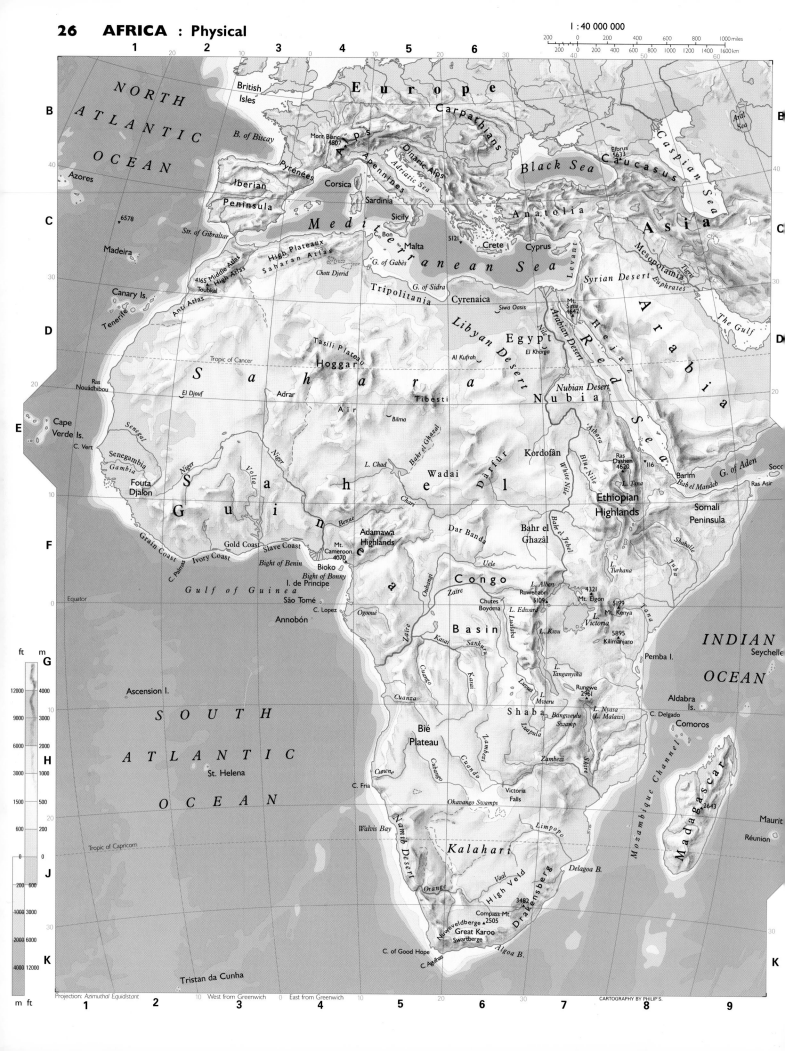

1 : 40 000 000

200   0   200   400   600   800   1000 miles
200   0   200   400   600   800 1000 1200 1400 1600 km

NORTH
ATLANTIC
OCEAN

British Isles

Europe

Carpathians

B. of Biscay

Mont Blanc 4807

ALPS

Dinaric Alps

Black Sea

Caucasus

Elbrus 5633

Aral Sea

Caspian Sea

B

Azores

Pyrénées

Apennines

Adriatic Sea

Anatolia

Asia

Iberian Peninsula

Corsica

Sardinia

Sicily

Crete

Cyprus

Mesopotamia

6578

C

Madeira

Str. of Gibraltar

Mediterranean Sea

C. Bon

Malta

5121

Levant

Syrian Desert

Tigris

Euphrates

The Gulf

Canary Is.

High Plateaux

Saharan Atlas

G. of Gabès

G. of Sidra

Tripolitania

Cyrenaica

Siwa Oasis

Mt. Sinai 4647

Arabian Desert

Red Sea

Hejaz

D

Tenerife

Anti Atlas

4165 Middle Atlas

High Atlas

Toubkal

Chott Djerid

Al Kufrah

Libyan Desert

Egypt

El Kharga

Nile

Arabia

Tasili Plateau

Tropic of Cancer

Ras Nouâdhibou

S   a   h   a   r   a

Hoggar

Adrar

Tibesti

Nubian Desert

Nubia

Ras Dashen 4620

116

Barim

Bab el Mandeb

G. of Aden

Ras Asir

Socc

E

Cape Verde Is.

C. Vert

El Djouf

Aïr

Bilma

Bahr el Ghazal

Darfûr

Kordofân

Albara

White Nile

Blue Nile

L. Tana

Senegal

Niger

Niger

Volta

S a h e l

L. Chad

Wadai

Chari

Ethiopian Highlands

Somali Peninsula

Senegambia

Gambia

Fouta Djalon

G u i n e a

Benue

Adamawa Highlands

Dar Banda

Bahr el Ghazâl

Bahr el Jebel

Shaballe

Juba

F

Grain Coast

Ivory Coast

C. Palmas

Gold Coast

Slave Coast

Bight of Benin

Mt. Cameroon 4070

Bioko

Uele

Ubangi

Congo

Zaïre

L. Albert

Ruwenzori 5109

4321

Mt. Elgon

5199

Mt. Kenya

Tana

Bight of Bonny

I. de Principe

São Tomé

Chutes Boyoma

L. Edward

L. Victoria

5895

Equator

Gulf of Guinea

C. Lopez

Ogooué

Zaïre

Basin

Kasai

L. Kivu

Kilimanjaro

INDIAN

Seychelle

0

Annobón

Luulaba

Lualaba

Sankuru

L. Tanganyika

Pemba I.

OCEAN

G

ft   m

12000 4000

Ascension I.

Cuango

Kasai

Lugenda

L. Mweru

Rungwe 2961

Aldabra Is.

9000 3000

SOUTH

Cuanza

Shaba

Bangweulu Swamp

L. Nyasa (L. Malawi)

C. Delgado

Comoros

6000 2000

ATLANTIC

Bié Plateau

Luapula

H

3000 1000

St. Helena

Zambezi

Cunene

Zambezi

Shire

1500 500

OCEAN

C. Fria

Cubango

Cuando

Victoria Falls

Mozambique Channel

Madagascar

2643

600 200

Tropic of Capricorn

Okavango Swamps

Maurit

0   0

Walvis Bay

Namib Desert

Kalahari

Limpopo

Réunion

J

200 600

Orange

Vaal

High Veld

Drakensberg

Delagoa B.

1000 3000

Nuweveldberge

Compass Mt 2505

3482

Algoa B.

2000 6000

C. of Good Hope

Great Karoo

Swartberge

4000 12000

C. Agulhas

K

m ft

Tristan da Cunha

Projection: Azimuthal Equidistant

West from Greenwich

East from Greenwich

CARTOGRAPHY BY PHILIP'S.

1 : 40 000 000

200   0   200   400   600   800   1000 miles
        0   200 400 600 800 1000 1200 1400 1600 km
        20

4   **5**   **6**   **7**   **8**   **9**   **10**

NORTH

ATLANTIC

OCEAN

B. of Biscay

UNITED
KINGDOM
LONDON
PARIS
FRANCE
NETH.
BELG.
GERMANY   POLAND   Warsaw
CZECH REP.   Prague   Kiev   RUSSIA
Vienna   SLOVAK REP.   UKRAINE   Volgograd   KAZAKSTAN
SWITZ.   AUSTRIA   HUNGARY   Odessa   GEORGIA   Aral
CROATIA   ROMANIA   Black Sea   ARM.   AZER.   Sea
BOS.-   YUG.   BULGARIA   GEORGIA   Baku   TURKMEN.
HERZ.   MAC.   Ankara   ARM.   Caspian Sea
ITALY   Adriatic Sea   GREECE   TURKEY   Mosul   TEHRÂN
Rome   Sardinia   Athens   CYPRUS   Aleppo   Baghdad   Eşfahân
Corsica   Sicily   Crete   SYRIA   Tigris   IRAN
MALTA   Damascus   Euphrates   Basra
Azores   Madrid   LEB.   IRAQ   KUWAIT
(Port.)   SPAIN   Tunis   Tel Aviv-Jaffa   Syrian Desert
Lisbon   Algiers   Annaba   Jerusalem   The Gulf
PORTUGAL   Constantine   ISRAEL   JORDAN
Rabat   Tétouan   TUNISIA   Tripoli   Benghazi   Alexandria   Port Said   SAUDI   BAHRAIN
Casablanca   Fès   Sfax   Misrâtah   CAIRO   Suez   QATAR
MOROCCO   Chott Djerid   El Faiyûm   Medina   Riyadh
Marrakesh   Asyût   ARABIA

Madeira
(Port.)   ALGERIA   LIBYA   EGYPT   Aswân   Jedda   Mecca
Canary Is.   In Salah   Al Jawf   Wadi Halfa   YEMEN
(Sp.)   Marzûq   Port Sudan
El Aaiún   Tropic of Cancer
Dakhla   WESTERN   Sahara   a   r   a   Atbara   Omdurmân
SAHARA   Fdérik   Khartoum   Asmera   ERITREA
Ras   MAURITANIA   Wâd Medani   Mesewa
Nouâdhibou   NIGER   CHAD   SUDAN   DJIBOUTI
VERDE IS.   Nouakchott   Tombouctou   Agadès   L. Chad   El-Fâsher   Djibouti   G. of Aden   Ras Asir
St-Louis   Senegal   NIGER   Abéché   El Obeid   Blue Nile   L. Tana   Socotra
C. Vert   Niamey   Kano   Ndjamena   White Nile   Berbera   (Yemen)
Praia   Dakar   SENEGAL   MALI   BURKINA   Maiduguri   Wau   Malakâl   Addis Ababa   Harer
GAMBIA   Banjul   Bamako   FASO   Ouagadougou   Chari   ETHIOPIA   SOMALI REP.
GUINEA-   Bissau   Bobo-   Benue   CENTRAL   Bahr el Jebel   L. Turkana   Mogadishu
BISSAU   GUINEA   Dioulasso   NIGERIA   AFRICAN REP.   Juba
Conakry   IVORY   GHANA   BENIN   Abuja   Enugu   Bangui   KENYA
Freetown   SIERRA   COAST   Kumasi   TOGO   Ibadan   Douala   Kisangani   UGANDA   Kisumu   INDIAN
LEONE   Yamoussoukro   Bouaké   Lomé   Lagos   Yaoundé   CAMEROON   Congo   Kampala   Nairobi
Monrovia   LIBERIA   Accra   Porto   Port   Malabo   GABON   Congo   L. Albert   L. Victoria   Kismayu
Abidjan   Sekondi-   Novo   Harcourt   EQUATORIAL   Libreville   CONGO   Mbandaka   RWANDA   L. Edward   OCEAN
Takoradi   Bight of Benin   GUINEA   SÃO TOMÉ & PRINCIPE   C. Lopez   GABON   Brazzaville   (DEM. REP. OF THE)   Kigali   Mombasa   SEYCHELLES
Equator   Gulf of Guinea   Annobón   Pointe Noire   Kinshasa   Kasai   BURUNDI   TANZANIA   Zanzibar
CABINDA   Matadi   Bujumbura   Dodoma   Dar es Salaam
(Angola)   Cuango   Kananga   L. Tanganyika   Aldabra
Ascension I.   Luanda   L. Mweru   Is.
(U.K.)   Lobito   ANGOLA   Likasi   L. Malawi   COMOROS
SOUTH   Huambo   Lúbumbashi   Ndola   C. Delgado   Mayotte
Namibe   ZAMBIA   Lilongwe   MALAWI   Moçambique   (Fr.)   Antsiranana
ATLANTIC   C. Fria   Cunene   Lusaka   Blantyre   MOZAMBIQUE   Mahajanga
St. Helena   Cubango   Zambezi   Harare   Beira   Toamasina
(U.K.)   Livingstone   ZIMBABWE   Antananarivo
OCEAN   Bulawayo   MADAGASCAR   MAURITIUS
NAMIBIA   Limpopo   Fianarantsoa   Réunion
Windhoek   BOTSWANA   (Fr.)
Tropic of Capricorn   Gaborone   Pretoria   Maputo
Johannesburg   Mbabane   SWAZ.
Kimberley   Vaal   Maseru   LESOTHO
Orange   SOUTH AFRICA   Durban
Cape Town   East
C. of Good Hope   Port   London
C. Agulhas   Elizabeth

Tristan da Cunha
(U.K.)

Projection: Azimuthal Equidistant   West from Greenwich   East from Greenwich   CARTOGRAPHY BY PHILIP'S

1   **2**   **3**   **4**   **5**   **6**   **7**   **8**   **9**

Dakar Capital Cities

NORTH ATLANTIC

OCEAN

SPAIN

NORTH ATLANTIC OCEAN

MOROCCO

WESTERN SAHARA

MAURITANIA

ALGERIA

MALI

NIGER

SENEGAL

GAMBIA

GUINEA-BISSAU

GUINEA

SIERRA LEONE

LIBERIA

IVORY COAST

BURKINA FASO

GHANA

TOGO

BENIN

NIGERIA

TUNISIA

Canary Is. (Sp.)

Madeira (Port.)

Anti Atlas

Saharan Atlas

Hoggar

El Djouf

Tanezrouft

Adrar des Iforhas

Aïr

Fouta Djalon

Lake Volta

Bight of Benin

Str. of Gibraltar

Gibraltar (U.K.)

Ceuta (Sp.)

Melilla (Sp.)

Cádiz • Málaga • Almería
Tangier • Tétouan • Al Hoceima
Larache • Ksar el Kebir
Kenitra • Salé • Rabat • Meknès • Fès • Taza
Casablanca
El Jadida • Berrechid • Khénifra
Settat • Khouribga
Safi • Beni Mellal
Marrakesh
Essaouira
Dj. Toubkal 4165
Agadir • Taroudannt
Ifni • Tiznit • Dra
Bou Izakarn
El Aaiún
Semara
Bu Craa
C. Bojador
Ain Ben Tili
Bir Mogrein
Chegga
Dakhla
C. Barbas
Fdérik • Zouérate
Châr
Nouâdhibou
Ras Nouâdhibou • La Güera
Atâr
Oujeft
Chinguetti
Ouadâne
Akjoujt
Rachid • Tidjikja
Tichît • Akreijit
Boutilimit
Moudjéria • Togba
Aleg
Tâmchekket
Néma
Ouâlâta
Oualâta
Nouakchott
Mederdra
Pador • Bogué
St. Louis
Rosso • Kaédi • Mbout
Louga • Dogana
Tivaouane • Dahra • Matam • Linguère
C. Vert • Thiès • Diourbel • Tiel
Dakar • Kaolack • Mbour
Kaffrine
Banjul • Georgetown
Sédhiou • Farim • Kolda
Ziguinchor • Bafatá
Bissau • Bolama
Gabú
Victoria • Boké
C. Verga • Boffa
Dubréka
Conakry
Télimélé • Pita • Dabola
Kindia • Mamou • Dinguiraye • Siguiri
Kankan
P. Loko • Forécariah • Kabala
Freetown • Waterloo
Sierra • Makeni
Moyamba • Bo • Kenema
Sherbro I. • Bonthe
Sulima • Robertsport
Monrovia • Careysburg
Marshall • Buchanan
River Cess
Greenville
Tindouf
Abadla
Béchar
Beni Abbès
Kerzaz
Timimoun
Adrar
In Belbel
Reggane
Zaouiet Reggane
Aoulef el Arab
In Salah
Arak
Ouallene
Bordj Omar Driss
Illizi
Bj.-Tarat
Tahat 2918
Tamanrasset
Idelès
Bj.-in-Eker
Poste Maurice Cortier
Djanet
Taoudenni
Terhazza
Taudenni
Mabrouk
Araouane
Bou Djébéha
Kidal
Timbedgha
Nioro du Sahel
Nara
Tombouctou
Goundam • Diré
Niafouké
Bamba • Bourem
Gourma-Rharous
Gaô • Ansongo
Ménaka
Kerchoual
I-n-Gall
Agadez
Iférouâne
Monts Tamgak
Aouderas
Hombori
Douentza
Mopti • Bandiagara
Djenné
Ségou
San
Bamako
Koulikoro
Kita • Kati
Bafoulabé • Kayes
Kédougou • Satadougou
Kéniéba
Faranah • Kissidougou
Beyla
Guéckédou • Macenta
Nzérékoré
Ganta
Man • Danané • Guiglo
Toulepleu • Tai
Tapeta
Gagnoa
Daloa • Bouaké
Yamoussoukro
Abidjan
Grand Bassam
Assinie
Sassandra
San-Pédro
Tabou
C. Palmas
Bouaflé
Séguéla • Bouaké
Katiola
Dabakala • Bouna
Bondoukou
Kumasi
Sekondi-Takoradi
Cape Coast
Accra
Lomé
Cotonou
Porto-Novo
Lagos
Abeokuta
Ibadan • Oyo • Ife • Ondo
Ado-Ekiti • Owo
Benin City
Onitsha • Enugu
Aba • Calabar
Port Harcourt
Warri • Sapele
Kano • Katsina • Zaria
Kaduna
Zinger • Maradi
Sokoto
Niamey • Dosso
Birnin-Kebbi
Ouagadougou
Bobo-Dioulasso
Tamale
Mont Cameroun 4070
Bioko
Douala

West from Greenwich   East from Greenwich

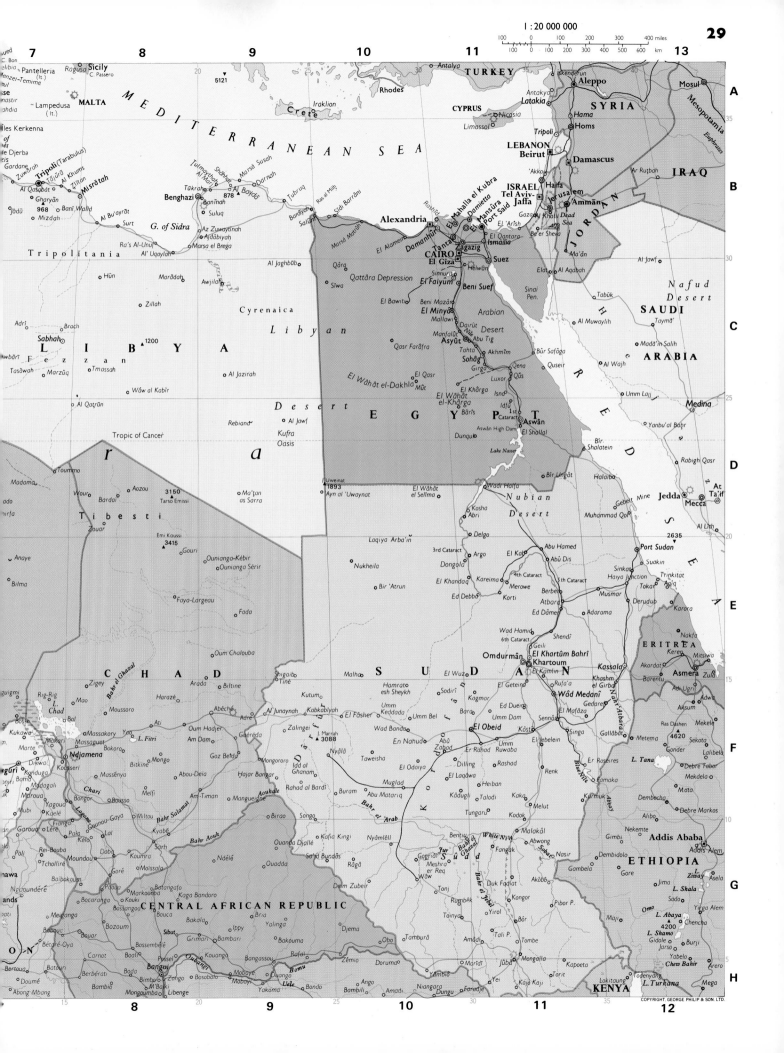

1 : 8 000 000

50   0   50   100   150   200 miles
50   0   50   100   200   300 km

CHAD

Lake Chad

N I G E R

M A L I

B U R K I N A   F A S O

I V O R Y   C O A S T

G H A N A

T O G O

B E N I N

N I G E R I A

C A M E R O U N

EQUATORIAL GUINEA

Gulf of Guinea

Bight of Benin

Niger Delta

Tombouctou (Timbuktu)
Gao
Niamey
Ouagadougou
Sokoto
Kano
Kano
Kaduna
Zaria
Maiduguri
BORNO
YOBE
BAUCHI
Bauchi
Jos
Plateau
ADAMAWA
Yola
Garoua
DOUALA
Yaoundé
IBADAN
LAGOS
Abeokuta
Benin City
Kumasi
ACCRA
Tema
Sekondi-Takoradi
Cape Coast
Lomé
Cotonou
Porto-Novo
Abomey
Parakou
Calabar
Port Harcourt
Enugu
Onitsha
Abuja
FED. CAP. TERR.
SOKOTO
KATSINA
JIGAWA
KEBBI
NIGER
KADUNA
BENUE
KOGI
OYO
OGUN
ONDO
EDO
DELTA
CROSS RIVER
ABIA
IMO
ANAMBRA
ENUGU
MO
BIOKO
Rey Malabo

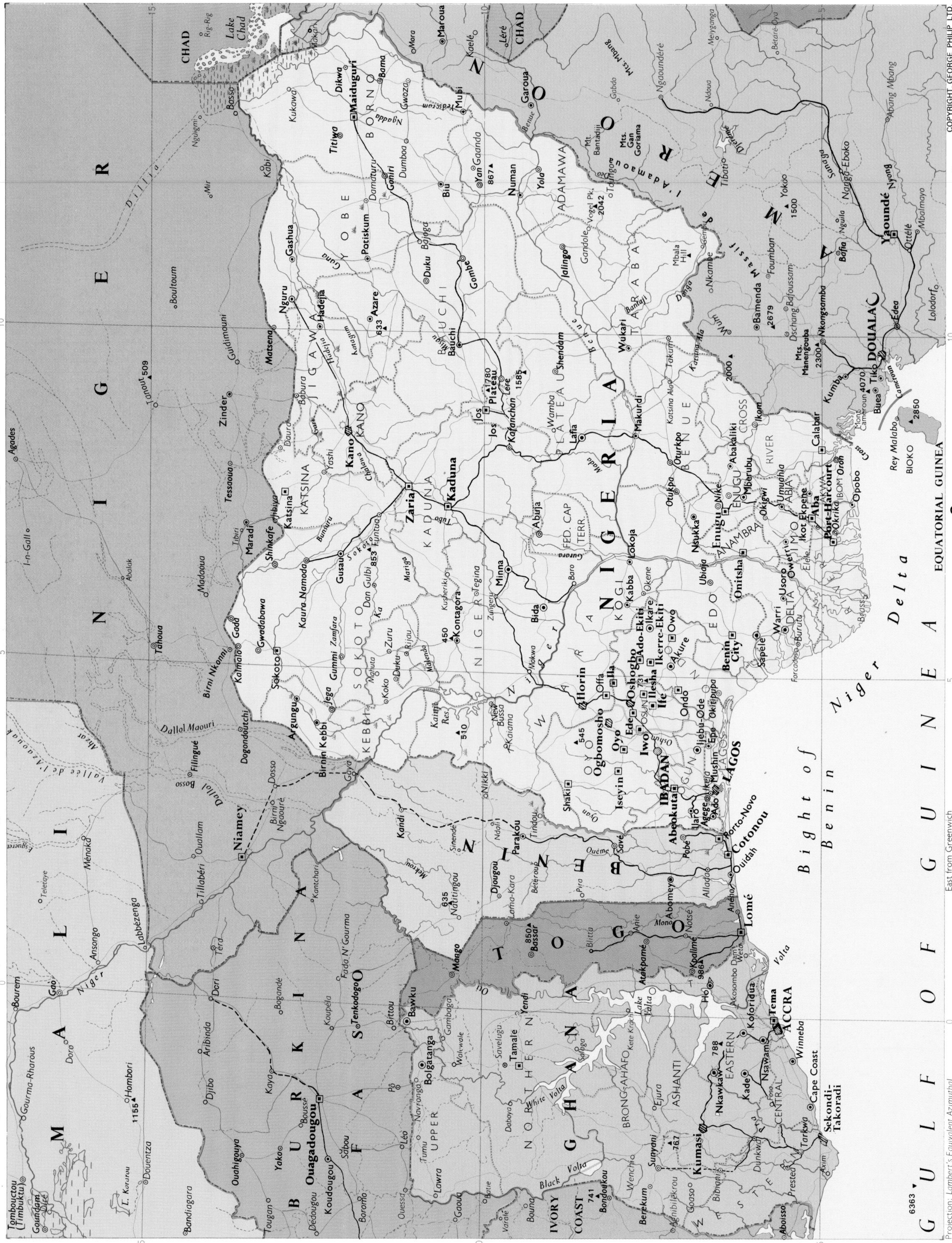

COPYRIGHT, GEORGE PHILIP LTD.

East from Greenwich

Projection: Lambert's Equivalent Azimuthal

A   B   C   D

1   2   3   4

1 : 8 000 000

MOZAMBIQUE

ZIMBABWE

NAMIBIA

BOTSWANA

SWAZI-LAND

LESOTHO

SOUTH AFRICA

NORTHERN PROVINCE

NORTH-WEST

GAUTENG

MPUMALANGA

FREE STATE

KWAZULU-NATAL

NORTHERN CAPE

EASTERN CAPE

WESTERN CAPE

Kalahari

Namib Desert

Great Karoo

Little Karoo

ATLANTIC OCEAN

INDIAN OCEAN

Tropic of Capricorn

PRETORIA

JOHANNESBURG

Bulawayo

Maputo

Pietermaritzburg

DURBAN

Bloemfontein

Kimberley

Kroonstad

Welkom

Port Elizabeth

East London

Umtata

Queenstown

Grahamstown

Upington

CAPE TOWN

Table Mt. 1086

C. of Good Hope

C. Agulhas

Windhoek

Walvis Bay

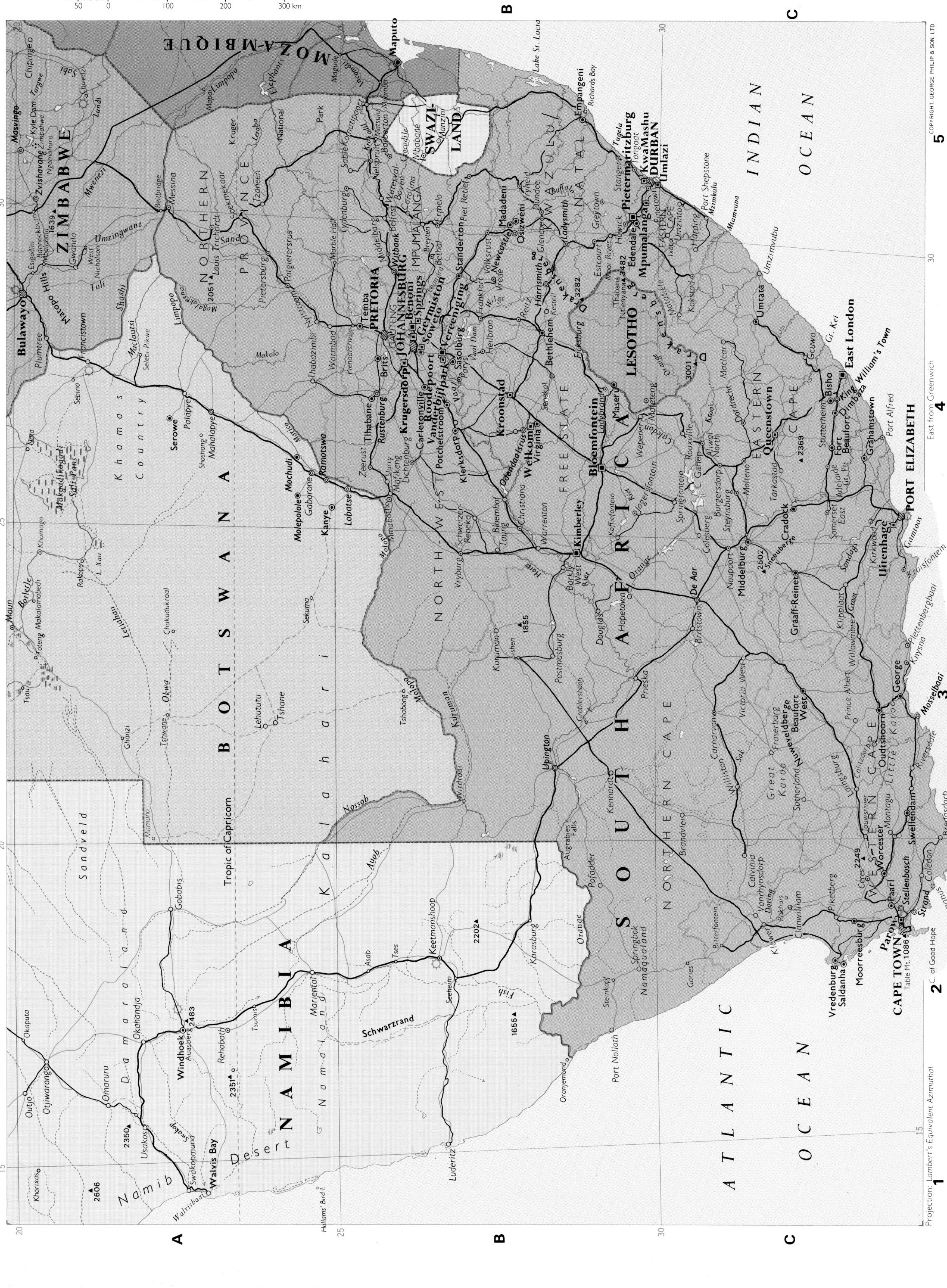

Projection: Lambert's Equivalent Azimuthal

East from Greenwich

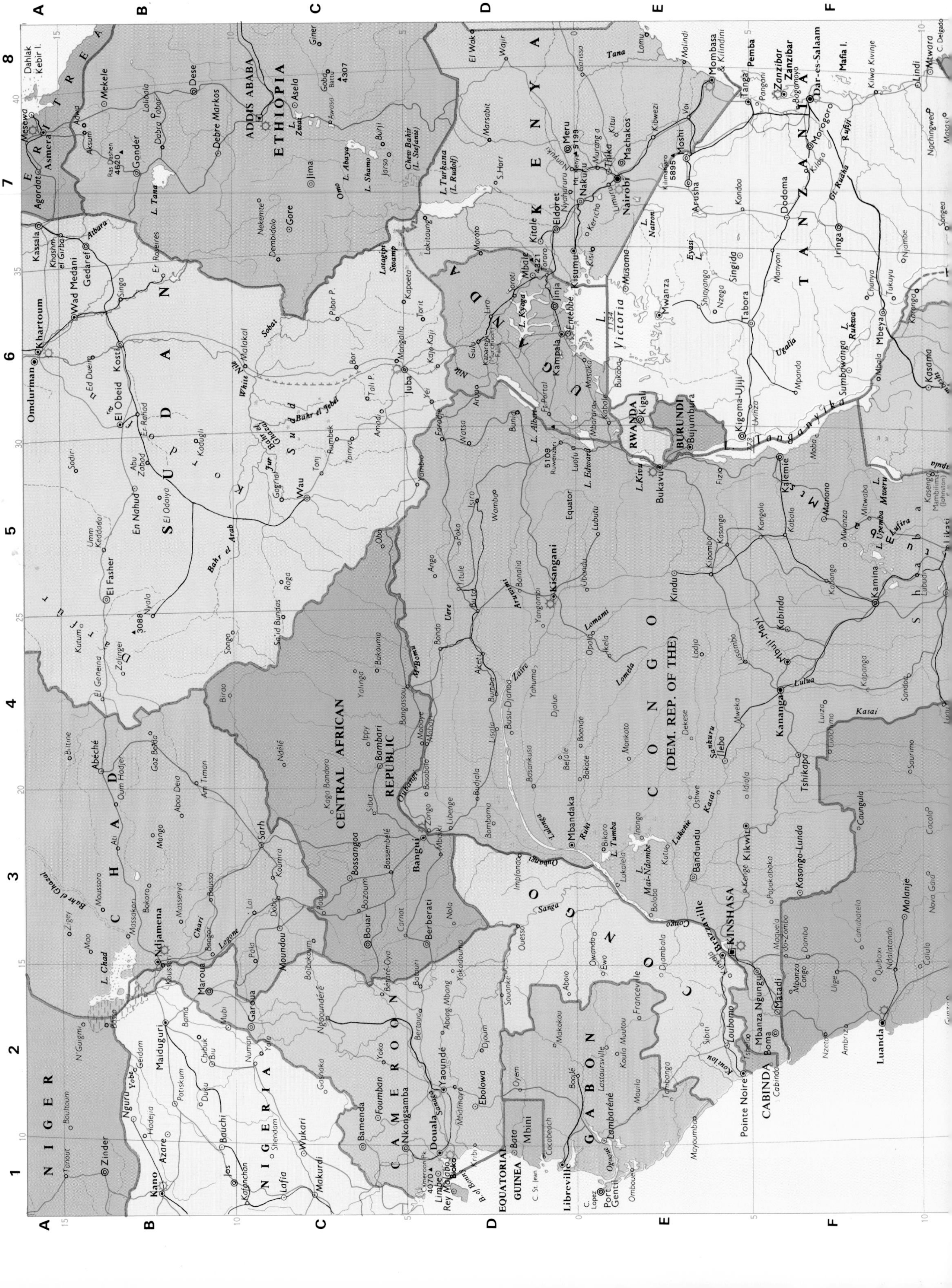

ETHIOPIA

ADDIS ABABA

SUDAN

KENYA

TANZANIA

UGANDA

RWANDA

BURUNDI

CONGO (DEM. REP. OF THE)

CENTRAL AFRICAN REPUBLIC

CHAD

CAMEROON

NIGERIA

NIGER

GABON

EQUATORIAL GUINEA

CABINDA

CONGO

Khartoum
Omdurman
Kassala
Gedaref
Wad Medani
El Obeid
El Fasher
Nyala
Kosti

Asmera
Mekele
Dese
Gonder
Debre Markos
Lalibala
Aksum

L. Tana
L. Zwai
Jima
Gore
Nekemte

Nairobi
Mombasa
Zanzibar
Dar-es-Salaam
Pemba
Mafia I.
Tanga
Moshi
Arusha
Dodoma
Iringa
Mbeya

L. Victoria
L. Turkana (L. Rudolf)
L. Tanganyika
L. Malawi
L. Kivu
L. Edward
L. Albert
L. Kyoga

Kampala
Entebbe
Jinja
Kigali
Bujumbura
Bukavu
Kalemie

Kisangani
Kananga
Kinshasa
Brazzaville
Mbandaka
Bandundu
Kikwit
Kindu
Kamina
Kabinda

Bangui
Bossangoa
Bouar
Berberati
Bambari
Ndélé

N'djamena
Sarh
Moundou
Abéché
Mongo
Ati

Maiduguri
Kano
Zinder

Yaoundé
Douala
Bamenda
Garoua
Maroua
Nkongsamba

Libreville
Port Gentil
Lambaréné
Franceville

Luanda
Mbanza Congo
Boma
Cabinda
Pointe Noire

Lake Chad

Ras Dashen 4620

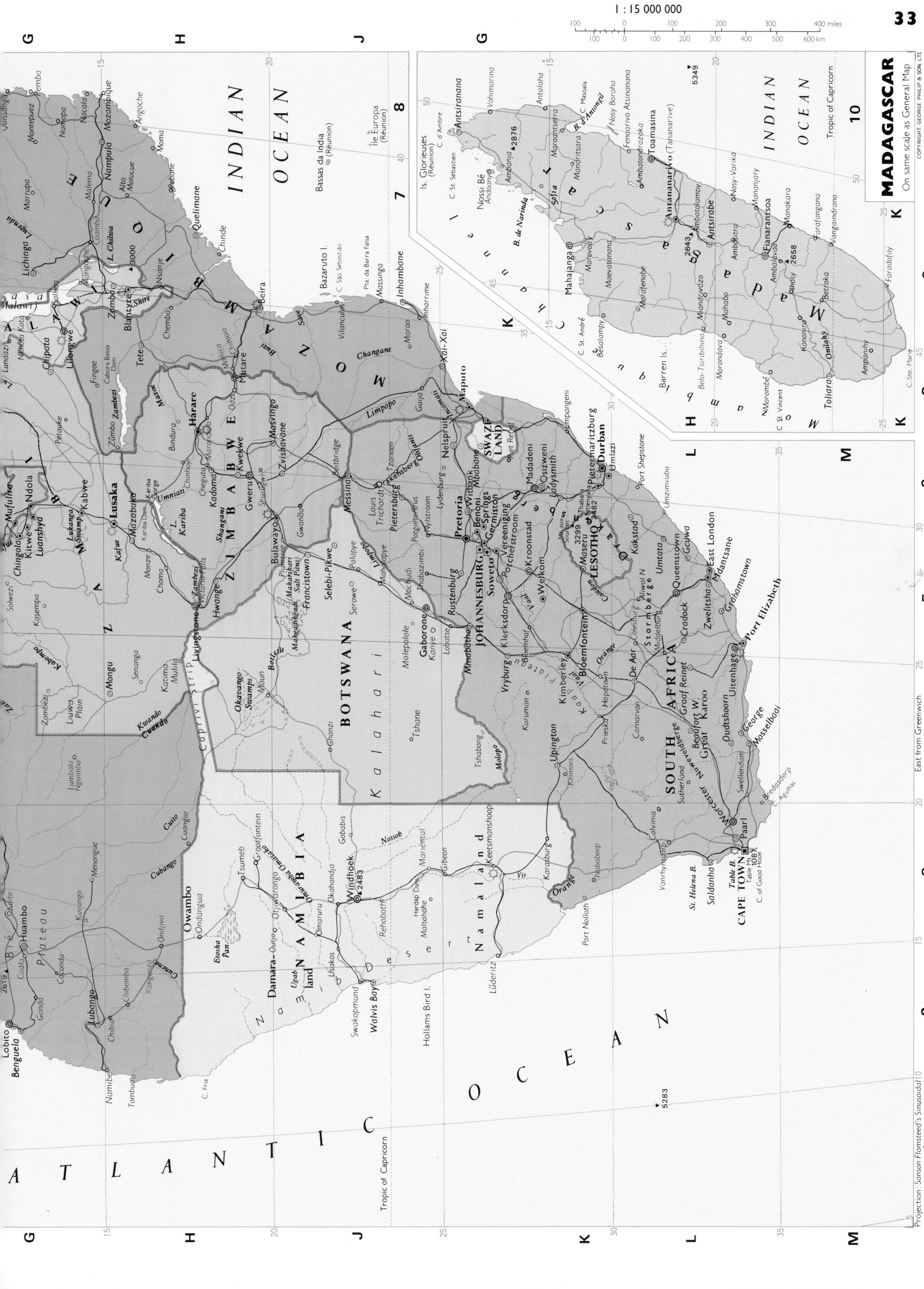
1 : 15 000 000
100 0 100 200 300 400 miles
100 0 100 200 300 400 500 600 km
MADAGASCAR
On same scale as General Map
COPYRIGHT GEORGE PHILIP & SON, LTD
INDIAN OCEAN
ATLANTIC OCEAN
Tropic of Capricorn
East from Greenwich
Projection: Sanson Flamsteed's Sinusoidal
ZAMBIA
ZIMBABWE
MOZAMBIQUE
BOTSWANA
NAMIBIA
SOUTH AFRICA
LESOTHO
SWAZILAND
Kalahari
Namaland
Caprivi Strip
Mozambique Channel
Lusaka
Harare
Bulawayo
Gaborone
Windhoek
Walvis Bay
Pretoria
JOHANNESBURG
Bloemfontein
Maseru
Durban
Pietermaritzburg
East London
Port Elizabeth
CAPE TOWN
Maputo
Beira
Inhambane
Antananarivo (Tananarive)
Toamasina
Mahajanga
Fianarantsoa
Toliara
Antsiranana
Limpopo
Zambezi
Orange
L. Kariba
L. Chilwa
Okavango Swamps
Etosha Pan
Bassas da India (Réunion)
Île Europa (Réunion)
Bazaruto I.
Is. Glorieuses (Réunion)
Hollams Bird I.
C. of Good Hope
C. Agulhas
C. Ste. Marie
5283
5349

Projection: *Lambert's Equivalent Azimuthal*

East from Greenwich

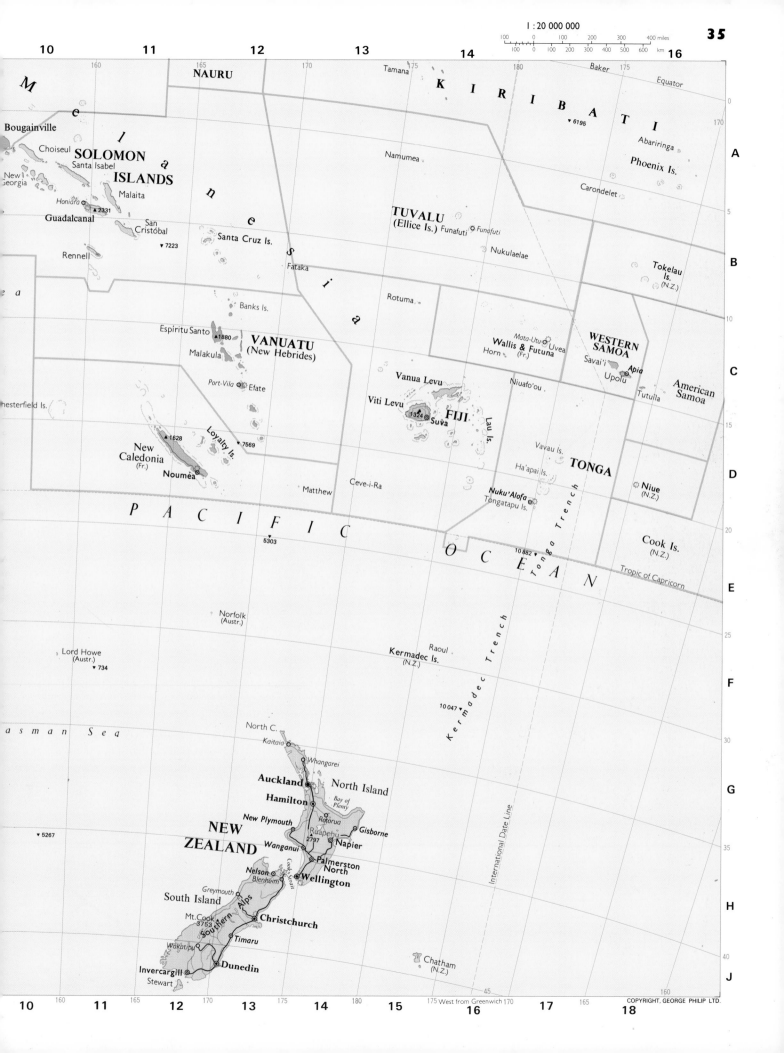

12 13 14 15 16 17 18 19 20

A L A S K A

GREENLAND

C. Farewell

NORTH

A

Gulf of Alaska
Prince of Wales I.
Prince Rupert
Queen Charlotte Is.
Kitimat
Juneau
▲5959

Hudson
Bay

ROCK C A N A D A

Edmonton

Labrador

B

Vancouver
Vancouver I.
Victoria
Seattle
Portland

N O R T H   A M E R I C A

Calgary
Regina
L. Winnipeg
Winnipeg

Newfoundland

50

NORTH

Montréal
Quebec
Pr. Edward I.
Saint John
C. Sable

C

L. Superior
Ottawa
Toronto
Boston

Mountains
Boise
Snake
Missouri

Minneapolis
CHICAGO
L. Huron
Michigan
Detroit
L. Erie
Buffalo
Pittsburgh
NEW YORK
Philadelphia

ATLANTIC

Salt Lake
City
▲4418

Denver
Kansas
St. Louis
Cincinnati
Baltimore
Washington

40

San Francisco

U N I T E D   S T A T E S

Oklahoma

C. Hatteras

D

Los Angeles
San Diego

Memphis
Atlanta

Jacksonville

Bermuda (U.K.)

6741

Ciudad
Juárez

Dallas
Mississippi
Appalachian Mts.

6225

Sierra Madre
M E X I
Gulf of California

San Antonio
Houston
New
Orleans

OCEAN

E

Hawaiian Is.
(U.S.)

Tropic of Cancer

Monterrey

Gulf of Mexico Miami
Florida Strait
BAHAMAS

30

Honolulu
Oahu

Havana
CUBA
West Indies

Hawaii
Revilla Gigedo Is.
(Mexico)
Guadalajara
Sierra Madre
México
Puebla ▲5700
Acapulco
7680
Yucatan Channel
Mérida
Hispaniola 9200
HAITI DOM.
JAMAICA REP.
Kingston
PUERTO
RICO
Leeward
Is.

20

I F I C

BELIZE
GUATEMALA
Guatemala ▲4066
HONDURAS
EL SALVADOR
NICARAGUA
Managua

Caribbean Sea

F

I. (U.S.)

BARBADOS
Windward
Is. TRINIDAD &
TOBAGO

Palmyra Is. (U.S.)
Teraina
Tabuaeran
Kiritimati

Clipperton I. (Fr.)

CENTRAL
AMERICA
COSTA RICA
San José
Panama
PANAMA
Canal
Barranquilla
Maracaibo
Caracas
VENEZUELA
Orinoco

10

G

Jarvis I.
(U.S.)

Cocos I.

Medellin
Bogota
Cali
COLOMBIA

E   A   N

Equator

Galápagos
(Ecuador)

Quito
ECUADOR

Manaus
Amazon

0

Malden I.
Starbuck I.

Guayaquil
Iquitos

BRAZIL

H

Marquesas Is.

C. Pariñas

SOUTH

Tongareva
Penrhyn Is.
Caroline I.
Vostok
I.
Flint I.

Trujillo

10

Manihiki
Suwarrow Is.

6369

PERU
Lima

AMERICA

Cook
Islands
(N.Z.)
Society Is.
Leeward Is.
Windward
Is.
Tahiti

Cuzco
L. Titicaca
Illampu & Ancohuma
6550

J

Rarotonga
FRENCH POLYNESIA
Tuamotu
Archipelago

Arequipa
▲6866
Peru-
La Paz
BOLIVIA

20

Tubuai Is.
(Austral Is.)

Austral

Seamount Chain

Mururoa
Pitcairn I. (U.K.)

Tropic of Capricorn

Iquique
Chile

8050
Antofagasta
Trench

PARAGUAY

K

Rapa Iti
Ducie I.
(U.K.)

Sala-y-Gomez
(Chile)
Easter Is.
(Chile)

San Félix (Chile)
San Ambrosio (Chile)

Asunción
Tucumán

East Pacific Ridge

Arch. de Juan Fernández
(Chile)
6960
Valparaíso
Santiago
Córdoba
Rosario
URUGUAY
Pto. Alegre

30

L

Buenos Aires
Montevideo

Concepción
ARGENTINA
Río de la Plata

SOUTH

40

Pacific-Antarctic Ridge

Chile Rise

ATLANTIC

M

Chonos Arch.
6212

OCEAN

G. of Penas
Punta Arenas
Str. of Magellan
Tierra del Fuego
C. Horn

Falkland Is. (U.K.)

South Georgia

50

N

1   2   3   4   5   6

A

BRITISH COLUMBIA
Vancouver I.
Str. of Georgia
Barkley Sd.
C. Flattery
Juan de Fuca Str.
Puget Sd.
Olympic Mts.
Vancouver
New Westminster
Victoria
Bellingham
Mt. Baker 3285
Everett
Seattle
Tacoma
Olympia
Mt. Rainier ▲4392
WASHINGTON
Cape Disappointment
Columbia
Yakima
Spokane
Coeur d'Alene
Pend Oreille L.
Columbia Basin
Upper Arrow Lake
Lower Arrow Lake
Kelowna
Kootenay Lake
Trail
Columbia
Mt. 3618
Selkirk Mts.
Rocky Mts.
Banff
Mt. Assiniboine
Calgary
ALBERTA   SASKATCHEWAN
Lethbridge
Bow
South Saskatchewan
Crowsnest Pass
Medicine Hat
Swift Current
Moose Jaw
Regina
Saskatoon
Last Mountain Lake
L. Winnipegosis
Lake Manitoba
MANI
Brandon
Assiniboine

B

Portland
Mt. Hood 3427
Salem
Eugene
Oregon
C. Blanco
Range
Coast
Bend
Blue Mountains
John Day
Pendleton
Walla Walla
Baker
Snake
Salmon
Columbia Plateau
IDAHO
Boise
Salmon Riv. Mts.
Bitterroot Range
Clark Fork
Missoula
Helena
Butte
Big Belt Mts.
Great Falls
MONTANA
Missouri
Havre
Milk
Fort Peck L.
Lake Sakakawea
Williston
Minot
NORTH DAKOTA
Bismarck
Jamestown
Little Missouri
Missouri
SOUTH DAKOTA
Grand
Lake Oahe
Aber

Vancouver
Columbia
Salmon
Snake
Owyhee
Harney Basin
Harney L.
Malheur L.
Summer L.
Upper Klamath L.
Klamath Falls
Medford
Klamath
Goose L.
Pit
▲Mt. Shasta 4317
C. Mendocino
Eureka
Redding
Lassen Pk. ▲3187
Twin Falls
Hyndman Pk. ▲3681
Idaho Falls
Pocatello
Yellowstone
Yellowstone National Park
Absaroka Range
Billings
Bighorn
Powder
Sheridan
Bighorn Mts.
WYOMING
Grand Teton ▲4196
Gannett Pk. ▲4202
Wind River Ra.
Wind
Casper

C

Sacramento
Santa Rosa
SAN FRANCISCO
Golden Gate
Oakland
San Jose
Stockton
Tahoe
Reno
Carson City
Carson Sink
Pyramid L.
Reese
Winnemucca
Elko
NEVADA
Great Salt Lake Desert
Great Salt Lake 1282
Ogden
Salt Lake City
Provo
Utah L.
Logan
Bear L.
Green
Rock Springs
Uinta Mts.
Yampa
White
Colorado
Fort Collins
Greeley
Laramie Mts.
Laramie
Cheyenne
Scottsbluff
North Platte
NEBRASKA
North Platte
Grand Island
Platte
Republican
Smoky Hills
Sal

Salinas
Walker Lake
Fresno
Yosemite National Park
White Mts.
Tonopah
Wheeler Pk. ▲3982
Sevier L.
Sevier
Wasatch
▲3710
Grand Junction
Gunnison
COLORADO
Mt. Elbert ▲4399
Sawatch Ra.
Park Range
Front Range
Denver
Colorado Springs
Pueblo
Arkansas
Smoky Hill
Garden City
Arkansas
Hutchi
KANSAS

D

Bakersfield
Tehachapi Pass
▲4418
Sequoia Nat. Park
Mt. Whitney
Death Valley -86
Santa Lucia Ra.
Santa Barbara
Coast Ranges
LOS ANGELES
Glendale
Long Beach
Anaheim
Santa Ana
San Bernardino
Riverside
Salton Sea
San Diego
Tijuana
Mexicali
Ensenada
Yuma
Mojave Desert ▲3505
Sonora Desert
CALIFORNIA
Las Vegas
Lake Mead
Zion Nat. Park
Grand Canyon Nat. Park
Grand Canyon
Painted Desert
Colorado Plateau
Humphreys Pk. ▲3851
Flagstaff
Colorado
Roof Butte 2989
San Juan
Durango
San Juan Mts.
Sangre de Cristo Mts.
Blanca Pk. ▲4378
Mt. Taylor ▲3445
Albuquerque
Santa Fe
Gallup
ARIZONA
Phoenix
Mesa
Gila
Verde
Baldy Pk. ▲3476
NEW MEXICO
Rio Grande
Clovis
Amarillo
Canadian
OKLA
Lawton
Liberal
North Canadian
Cimarron
Enid
Wichi

E

San Diego
Tijuana
Mexicali
Ensenada
BAJA CALIFORNIA
Sebastian Vizcaino B.
I. Cedros
Guadalupe I.
Lower California
Gulf of California
BAJA CALIFORNIA SUR
▲3078
Tucson
Nogales
Los Cruces
Santa Blanca ▲3659
Alamogordo
Sacramento Mts.
San Andres Mts.
Black Ra.
Gila
Pecos
Roswell
Estacado
Llano
Carlsbad
Hobbs
El Paso
Ciudad Juarez
Sierra Madre
SONORA
Hermosillo
Sonora
Yaqui
Conchos
Rio Grande
CHIHUAHUA
Chihuahua
Del Rio
Odessa
Midland
San Angelo
TEXAS
Colorado
Pecos
Edwards Plateau
Abilene
Fort Wo
Lubbock
Brazos
San Anto

G / H / J (HAWAII inset)

Kauai
Lihue
Niihau
Kauai Channel
Oahu
Honolulu
Kaiwi Channel
Molokai
Lanai
Maui
Lahaina
Haleakala ▲3055
PACIFIC OCEAN
Hawaiian Islands
Alenuihaha Channel
Hawaii
Mauna Kea ▲4205
Mauna Loa ▲4169
Hilo
Kilauea Crater
Hawaiian Channel

HAWAII
1 : 10 000 000
20 0 20 40 60 80 miles
20 0 40 80 120 km
Projection: Albers' Equal Area with two standard parallels

Guaymas
Ciudad Obregon
Los Mochis
Fuerte
Conchos
Bolson de Mapimi
▲3348
DURANGO
Gomez Palacio
Torreon
Hidalgo del Parral
MEXICO
COAHUILA
Piedras Negras
Eagle Pass
Nuevo Rosita
Monclova
Nuevo Laredo
Laredo
Salado
Monterrey
Matamore
Gulf of California

PACIFIC OCEAN

105   6
16   17   4   5

1 2 3 4 5 6 7 8 9

A

B

C

D

E

F

G

CANADA

ONTARIO

QUEBEC

Lake Nipigon
Thunder Bay
Isle Royale
Grand Marais

LAKE SUPERIOR

Duluth
Superior
Ashland
Hurley Ironwood
Bessemer
Hancock
Houghton
Keweenaw Pen.
Keweenaw Pt.
Copper Harbor
Keweenaw B.
Whitefish Pt.
Sault Ste. Marie

Hearst
Kapuskasing
Hornepayne
Nakina
Geraldton
Longlac
Nipigon
Schreiber
Atikokan
Lac la Croix
Ignace

Timmins
Cochrane
Noranda Rouyn
Kirkland Lake
Val d'Or
La Sarre
Amos
Abitibi L.
Matagami L.
Matagami

Michipicoten I.
Wawa
Chapleau
Gogama
New Liskeard
Haileybury
Ville-Marie
Temiscaming
Deep River
Pembroke

MICHIGAN

Marquette
Negaunee
Ishpeming
Munising
Newberry
St. Ignace
Mackinaw City
Cheboygan
Petoskey
Rogers City
Alpena
Thunder B.
Manistique
Escanaba
Pt. Detour
Beaver I.
Charlevoix
Gaylord
Mancelona
Kalkaska
Traverse City
Frankfort
Grayling
Au Sable
Harrisville
Roscommon
Houghton W.
Manton
Cadillac
Manistee
Ludington
Baldwin
Hart
Big Rapids
Mount Pleasant
Midland
Bay City
Saginaw
Alma
Standish
Gladwin
Harbor Beach
Bad Axe
Goderich
Cass City
Caro
Pigeon
Tawas City
Pte. aux Barques
Saginaw Bay

LAKE HURON

North Channel
Manitoulin I.
Little Current
Cockburn I.
Drummond I.
Thessalon
Blind River
Spanish
Sudbury
Capreol
Coniston
Sturgeon Falls
North Bay
Nipissing
Mattawa
Georgian Bay
Parry Sound
Tobermory
Wiarton
Owen Sound
Meaford
Penetanguishene
Midland
Orillia
Collingwood
Barrie
Port Elgin
Kincardine
Walkerton
Hanover
Listowel
Orangeville
Brampton
Guelph
Kitchener
Waterloo
Stratford
Woodstock
Brantford
Hamilton
Oshawa
Oakville
Huntsville
Bracebridge
Gravenhurst
Bancroft
Bobcaygeon
Marmora
Lindsay
Peterborough
Belleville
Trenton
Picton
Cobourg

TORONTO

LAKE ONTARIO

Niagara Falls
St. Catharines
Welland
Niagara Falls
Buffalo
West Seneca
Rochester
Newark
Batavia
Canandaigua
Seneca
Penn Yan
Amherst

WISCONSIN

Two Harbors
Apostle Is.
Washburn
Ontonagon
L'Anse
Spooner
Hayward
Rice Lake
Ladysmith
Phillips
Rhinelander
Eagle River
Crandon
Antigo
Merrill
Medford
Tomahawk
Wausau
Stevens Point
Waupaca
Shawano
Oconto
Marinette
Menominee
Sturgeon Bay
Green Bay
De Pere
Kewaunee
Appleton
Kaukauna
Menasha
Neenah
Oshkosh
Fond du Lac
Sheboygan
Manitowoc
Two Rivers
Chippewa Falls
Eau Claire
Menomonie
Cornell
Marshfield
Wisconsin Rapids
Black River Falls
Whitehall
Sparta
La Crosse
Tomah
Wautoma
Ripon
Waupun
Beaver Dam
West Bend
Port Washington
Plymouth
Hartford
Watertown
Madison
Portage
Baraboo
Reedsburg
Richland Center
Prairie du Chien
Dodgeville
Lancaster
Darlington
Monroe
Janesville
Whitewater
Waukesha
Wauwatosa

MILWAUKEE

Racine
Kenosha
Waukegan
Dubuque
Freeport
Rockford
Belvidere
Beloit

LAKE MICHIGAN

Frankfort
Green Bay

ILLINOIS

Galena
Maquoketa
Davenport
Rock Island
Moline
Aledo
Kewanee
Galesburg
Monmouth
Peoria
Pekin
Canton
Macomb
Rushville
Beardstown
Jacksonville
Springfield
Taylorville
Carlinville
Pana
Litchfield
Shelbyville
Carrollton
Jerseyville
Alton
Granite City
Belleville

ST. LOUIS

St. Charles
Vandalia
Effingham
Mattoon
Charleston
Flora
Olney
Centralia
Fairfield
Mount Carmel
Mount Vernon
Nashville
Waterloo
Pinckneyville
Du Quoin
Benton
Marion
Carbondale
Murphysboro
Anna
Cape Girardeau
Charleston
Cairo
Paducah
Metropolis
Sikeston
New Madrid
Hickman
Union City
Murray
Mayfield
L. Barkley

Rockford
De Kalb
Elgin
Skokie
Evanston
Cicero

CHICAGO

Aurora
Joliet
Harvey
Gary
Hammond
South Bend
Elkhart
Mishawaka
La Porte
Morris
Ottawa
Streator
Pontiac
Kankakee
Watseka
Hoopeston
Normal
Bloomington
Lincoln
Clinton
Champaign
Urbana
Danville
Decatur
Paxton
Rantoul
Lafayette
Frankfort
Crawfordsville

INDIANA

Fort Wayne
Auburn
Warsaw
Plymouth
Rochester
Peru
Wabash
Huntington
Marion
Kokomo
Logansport
Delphos
Lima
Kenton
Celina
Van Wert
Muncie
Anderson
Lebanon
Noblesville
Indianapolis
Greencastle
Brazil
Terre Haute
Martinsville
Bloomington
Linton
Vincennes
Washington
Bedford
Jasper
Princeton
Evansville
Boonville
Tell City
Owensboro
Henderson

New Castle
Richmond
Connersville
Greenfield
Rushville
Greensburg
Shelbyville
Columbus
Seymour
North Vernon
Madison
Scottsburg
New Albany
Jeffersonville

OHIO

Toledo
Bowling Green
Bryan
Napoleon
Defiance
Fremont
Sandusky
Lakewood
Lorain
Euclid

CLEVELAND

Elyria
Norwalk
Tiffin
Fostoria
Findlay
Bucyrus
Marion
Mansfield
Ashland
Wooster
Akron
Barberton
Canton
Massillon
Warren
Youngstown
Salem
Alliance
New Philadelphia
Coshocton
Mount Vernon
Delaware
Urbana
Bellefontaine
Sidney
Greenville
Troy
Piqua
Dayton
Springfield
Xenia
Middletown
Hamilton
Kettering
Wilmington

CINCINNATI

Newport
Covington
Maysville
Washington C.H.
Chillicothe
Circleville
Lancaster
New Lexington
Logan
Athens
Marietta
Parkersburg
Portsmouth
Gallipolis
Ironton
Ashland

COLUMBUS

Newark
Zanesville
Cambridge
Bellaire
Wheeling
Moundsville
Steubenville
McKeesport
Washington

PENNSYLVANIA

Meadville
Titusville
Oil City
Franklin
Sharon
New Castle
Butler
Beaver Falls
Aliquippa

PITTSBURGH

Penn Hills
Greensburg
Johnstown
Indiana
Altoona
State College
Lewistown
Kittanning
Punxsutawney
Du Bois
Clearfield
Lock Haven
Williamsport
Sunbury
Kane
Ridgway
St. Marys
Emporium
Brookville
Coudersport
Wellsboro
Towanda
Corry
Warren
Erie
Conneaut
Ashtabula
Painesville
Jamestown
Salamanca
Olean
Bradford
Hornell
Corning
Bath
Wellsville

WEST VIRGINIA

Morgantown
Waynesburg
Uniontown
Connellsville
Clarksburg
Fairmont
Weston
Buckhannon
Elkins
Spencer
Charleston
South Charleston
Huntington
St. Albans
Point Pleasant
Oak Hill
Logan
Williamson
Beckley
Hinton
Webster Springs
Welch
Bluefield
Princeton
Richwood
Clifton Forge
Buena Vista

KENTUCKY

Louisville
Frankfort
Lexington
Georgetown
Winchester
Nicholasville
Danville
Harrodsburg
Lebanon
Bardstown
Elizabethtown
Bowling Green
Glasgow
Campbellsville
Somerset
Jamestown
Monticello
Corbin
Hazard
Pikeville
Paintsville
Salyersville
Jackson
Morehead
Mount Sterling
Louisa
Wayne
Berea
Russellville
Hopkinsville
Princeton
Madisonville
Hartford

VIRGINIA

MARYLAND

WASHINGTON D.C.

BALTIMORE

Cumberland
Hagerstown
Martinsburg
Keyser
Romney
Winchester
Front Royal
Luray
Harrisonburg
Staunton
Charlottesville
Waynesboro
Lexington
Lynchburg
Bedford
Roanoke
Salem
Blacksburg
Radford
Richlands
Hinton
Culpeper
Fredericksburg
Orange
Arlington
Alexandria
Frederick
Columbia
York
Hanover
Chambersburg
Carlisle
Harrisburg
Lewistown

PHILADELPHIA

Richmond
Petersburg
Colonial Heights
Lakeside
Tappahannock
Farmville

LAKE ERIE

Detroit
Windsor
Ann Arbor
Monroe
Ypsilanti
Inkster
Livonia
Warren
Sterling Heights
Pontiac
Flint
Lapeer
Port Huron
Sarnia
Strathroy
London
St. Thomas
Simcoe
Wallaceburg
Chatham
Leamington
Dunkirk
Fredonia

MICHIGAN
Jackson
Albion
Battle Creek
Kalamazoo
Benton Harbor
St. Joseph
Hillsdale
Adrian
Coldwater
Sturgis
Three Rivers
Niles
Dowagiac
Holland
Grand Haven
Muskegon
Grand Rapids
Wyoming
Greenville
Ionia
Lansing
East Lansing
Charlotte
Howell
Owosso
St. Johns
Allegan
Hastings

1 : 6 000 000

50   0   50   100   150 miles
50   0   50   100   150   200 km

10   11   12   13   14

D   A   556 ▲ Chibougamau Chibougamau L.   Pipmuacan L.   Port-Cartier   West Pt.   A n t i c o s t i   I.   Jupiter   Heath Pt.   62   60   A

48

Gouin   Dolbeau   Péribonca   Cap-Chat   1310   Gaspé   C. Gaspé   GULF OF   ▼ 572
Res.   St. Félicien   Lac   Saguenay   Matane   Shickshock Mts.   ST. LAWRENCE
Roberval   St. Jean   Chicoutimi   Gaspé Peninsula

Jonquière   Rimouski   Dalhousie   Chaleur Bay   Magdalen   C. North   B
B   La Tuque   Rivière du Loup   Campbellton   Bathurst   Is.   532   Cape Breton
E   C   Baie St. Paul   Edmundston   819 ▲   N E W   Newcastle   (Quebec)   North Pt.   Tignish   PRINCE EDWARD   Island
L'Annonciation   Fort   Van   Grand   Miramichi B.   North Pt.   ISLAND   Glace Bay
Grand-Mère   Ste-Marie   Kent Buren   Falls   B R U N S W I C K   Chatham   Summerside   East Pt.   Sydney
Shawinigan   Québec   Île d'Orléans   Eagle   Caribou   Chipman   Charlottetown   Bras d'Or
Cap-de-la-Madeleine   Louzon   Lake   Northumberland Str.   L.
968 ▲ Trois-Rivières   Lévis   Presque Isle   Houlton   Moncton   Springhill   New Glasgow   Chédabucto B.
Louiseville   Plessisville   Chamberlain   Grand L.   Fredericton   Stellarton   Canso
Joliette   Victoriaville   St-George   L.   Patten   Sussex   Truro   N   Dartmouth   C
St-   Thetford   Chesuncook   1605   Millinocket   Chiputneticook   Saint   Kentville   O
Jérôme   Sorel   Drummondville   Mines   L.   Mt. Katahdin   Lakes   John   V   Halifax
Hawkesbury   St-   Asbestos   Moosehead   Lincoln   St. Stephen   Bay of Fundy   A   Bridgewater
MONTREAL   Hyacinthe   Lac-   L.   Greenville   Mattawamkeag   Galais   Digby   S   44
Ottawa   Lachine   Granby   Mégantic   Dover   St. Stephen   East-   C   Rossignol Res.   Shelburne
Cornwall   St-Jean   Sherbrooke   Foxcroft   Old Town   port   O   C. Sable
Beauharnois   Magog   Coaticook   Richardson   M A I N E   Brewer   Grand   Yarmouth   T
Cowansville   Lakes   Bangor   Manan I.   I
Malone   Newport   Island Pond   Dover-   Machias   A
Massena   St. Albans   Farmington   Skowhegan   Ellsworth   Bar
Plattsburg   Rangeley   Waterville   Harbor   Mt. Desert
Potsdam   Champlain   Winooski   Berlin   Rumford   Augusta   Belfast
Canton   Burlington   St.   1917   Gardiner   Penobscot B.
Ogdensburg   Montpelier   Barre   White   Mts.   Lewiston   Rockland
Saranac Lakes   Middlebury   Mt.   Auburn   Bath
Gouverneur   1629   Johnsbury   Washington   Conway   Brunswick
Watertown   Adirondack Mts.   Ticonderoga   Lancaster   Westbrook   Portland
Lowville   L. George   V E R M O N T   Conway   Saco
Lake Pleasant   Rutland   Lebanon   Laconia   Biddeford
Rome   Claremont   Franklin   Rochester
Utica   Glens   Hudson   Springfield   Concord   Dover
Gloversville   Falls   Keene   Manchester   Portsmouth
Oneida   Amsterdam   Saratoga Springs   Brattleboro   Nashua   Haverhill
Syracuse   Schenectady   Troy   Greenfield   Fitchburg   Lawrence   C. Ann   42
York   Norwich   Albany   Pittsfield   Leominster   Lowell
Oneonta   Catskill   M A S S.   Cambridge   Salem
Cortland   Binghamton   Mts.   Northampton   Worcester   BOSTON
Johnson City   Catskill   1281   Chicopee   Quincy   Cape Cod
Binghamton   Kingston   Springfield   Woonsocket   Brockton
Carbondale   Poughkeepsie   Hartford   Pawtucket   Taunton
Dunmore   Newburgh   Waterbury   New Britain   Providence   Fall River
Wilkes   Middletown   Beacon   C O N N. R. I.   Warwick   New
Barre   Danbury   New   Meriden   Newport   Bedford
Hazelton   Paterson   Bridgeport   Haven   New   Martha's
Shandoah   Easton   Jersey City   Stamford   London   Vineyard   Nantucket
Bethlehem   Newark   Yonkers   Mount   Block I.
town   Reading   Elizabeth   Vernon   Long Island
NEW YORK   Riverhead
Philadelphia   Norristown   New Brunswick   Long Branch   40
PHIA   Trenton   Asbury Park
Camden   NEW
Chester   JERSEY
ter   Wilmington   Hammonton   F
Bridgeton   Vineland
Millville   Atlantic City
Dover   Ocean City
Cape May
Milford   C. Henlopen   A T L A N T I C   38
is   DELAWARE
Cambridge   O C E A N
bury
Snow Hill   G
Accomac
Cape Charles
C. Charles

West from Greenwich

10   74   11   72   12   70   13   68   14   66   15   64   16

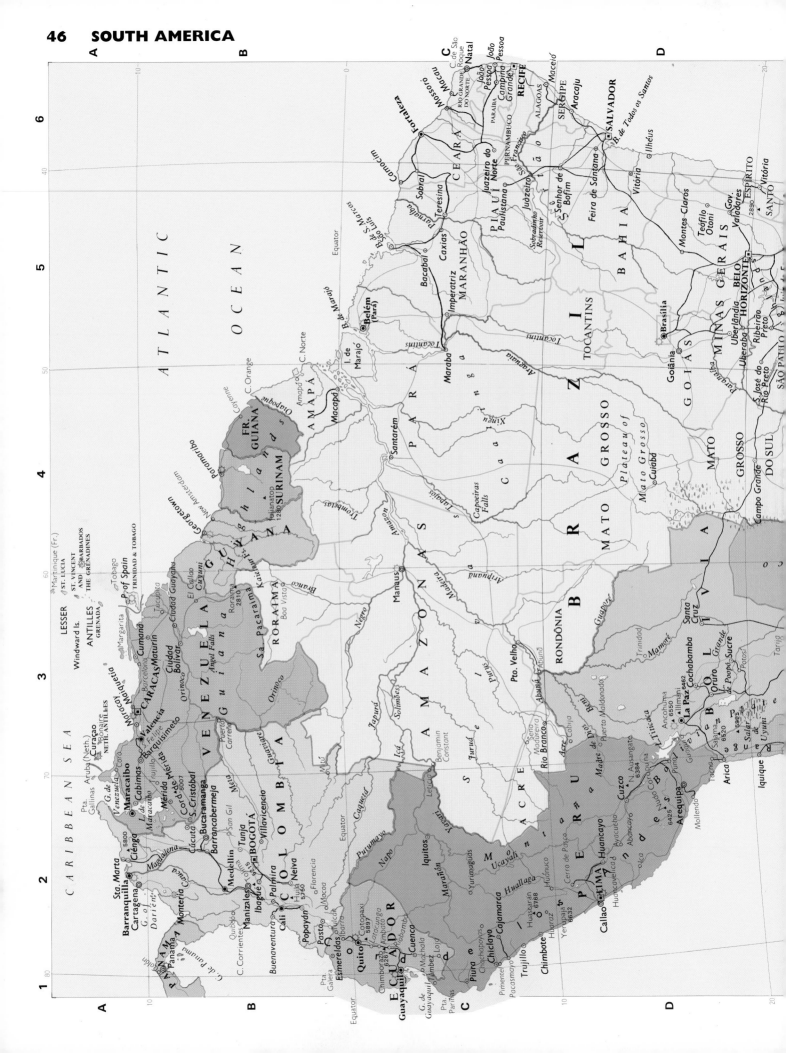

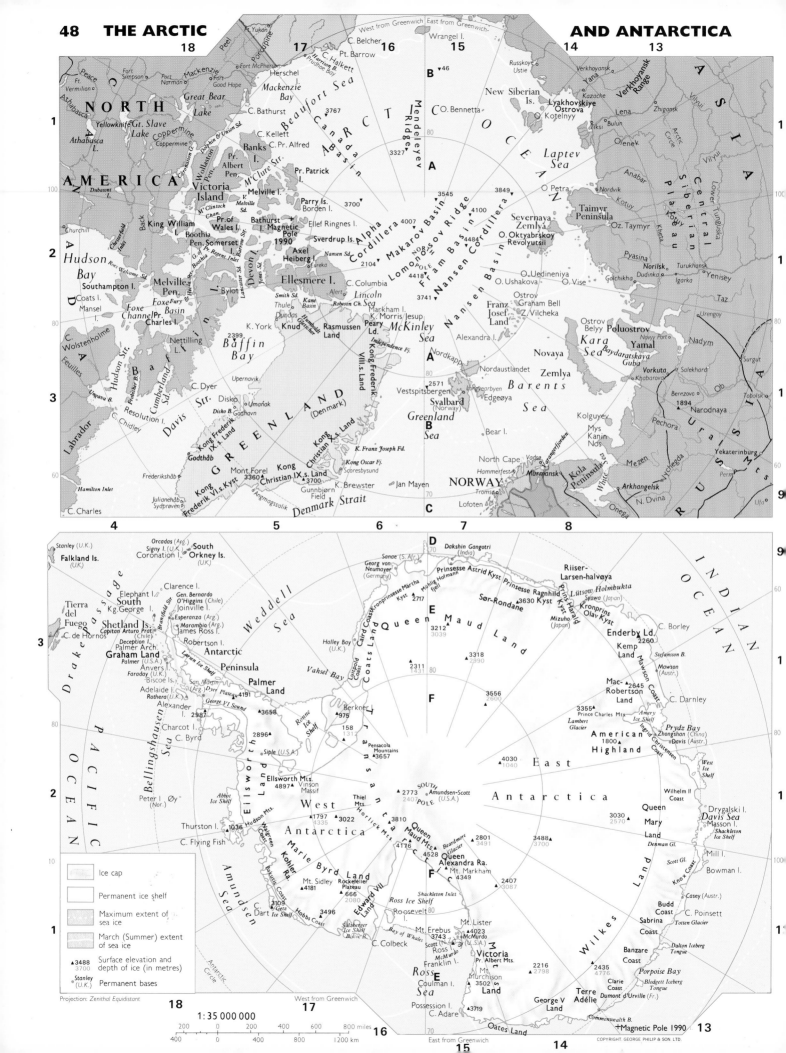

INDEX

The index contains the names of all the principal places and features shown on the maps. The alphabetical order of names composed of two or more words is governed primarily by the first word and then by the second. This is an example of the rule:

New South Wales □ 34 G8
New York □ 43 D9
New York City 43 E11
New Zealand ■ 35 J13
Newark, Del., U.S.A. 43 F10

Physical features composed of a proper name (Erie) and a description (Lake) are positioned alphabetically by the proper name. The description is positioned after the proper name and is usually abbreviated:

Erie, L. 42 D7

Where a description forms part of a settlement or administrative name, however, it is always written in full and put in its true alphabetical position:

Mount Isa 34 E6

Names beginning with M' and Mc are indexed as if they were spelt Mac. Names beginning St. are alphabetized under Saint, but Santa and San are all spelt in full and are alphabetized accordingly. If the same placename occurs two or more times in the index and all are in the same country, each is followed by the name of the administrative subdivision in which it is located. The names are placed in the alphabetical order of the subdivision. For example:

Columbus, Ga., U.S.A. 41 D10
Columbus, Ind., U.S.A. 42 F5
Columbus, Ohio, U.S.A. 42 F6

The number in bold type which follows each name in the index refers to the number of the map page where that feature or place will be found. This is usually the largest scale at which the place or feature appears.

The letter and figure which are in lighter type immediately after the page number give the grid square on the map page, within which the feature is situated. The letter represents the latitude and the figure the longitude. In some cases the feature itself may fall within the specified square, while the name is outside.

Rivers are indexed to their mouths or confluences, and carry the symbol → after their names. A solid square ■ follows the name of a country, while an open square □ refers to a first order administrative area.

Belonia 23 H13
Belorussia = Belarus ■ 11 B14
Beltsy 11 E14
Belukha 18 E10
Ben Nevis 7 C4
Benares = Varanasi 23 G9
Bendigo 34 H7
Benevento 12 D6
Bengal, Bay of 23 K12
Bengbu 21 C6
Benghazi 29 B9
Bengkulu 22 D2
Beni Suef 29 C11
Benidorm 9 C5
Benin ■ 30 C2
Benin, Bight of 30 C2
Benin City 30 C3
Benoni 31 B4
Benton Harbor 42 D4
Benue → 30 C3
Benxi 21 B7
Berbérati 32 D3
Berea 42 G5
Bérgamo 12 B3
Bergen 6 F9
Bergerac 8 D4
Berhala Str. 22 D2
Berhampur 23 K10
Bering Sea 36 B9
Bering Strait 38 B3
Berlin, Germany 10 B7
Berlin, U.S.A. 43 C12
Bermuda ■ 45 A12
Berne 10 E4
Berry 8 C5
Berwick 42 E9
Berwick-upon-Tweed 7 D5
Besançon 8 C7
Bethal 31 B4
Bethlehem, S. Africa 31 B4
Bethlehem, U.S.A. 43 E10
Béthune 8 A5
Bettiah 23 F10
Betul 23 J6
Béziers 8 E5
Bhagalpur 23 G11
Bhandara 23 J7
Bhanrer Ra. 23 H7
Bharatpur 23 F6
Bhatinda 23 D5
Bhatpara 23 H12
Bhavnagar 23 J4
Bhilwara 23 G5
Bhima → 25 D6
Bhiwani 23 E6
Bhopal 23 H6
Bhubaneshwar 23 J10
Bhuj 23 H2
Bhusaval 23 J5
Bhutan ■ 23 F13
Biafra, B. of 26 F4
Biała Podlaska 11 B12
Białystok 11 B12
Biarritz 8 E3
Biddeford 43 D12
Bié Plateau 33 G3
Biel 10 E4
Bielefeld 10 B5
Bielsko-Biała 11 D10
Bien Hoa 22 B2
Big Rapids 42 D5
Bighorn Mts. 40 B5
Bihar 23 G10
Bihar □ 23 G10
Bikaner 23 E4
Bikini Atoll 36 F8
Bilaspur 23 H9
Bilbao 9 A4
Billings 40 A5
Bina-Etawah 23 G7
Binghamton 43 D10
Binjai 22 C1
Bioko 30 D3
Birmingham, U.K. 7 E6
Birmingham, U.S.A. 41 D9
Biscay, B. of 8 D1
Bishkek 18 E9
Bisho 31 C4
Biskra 28 B6
Bismarck Arch. 34 A9
Bissau 28 F1
Bitolj 13 D9
Bitterfontein 31 C2
Biwa-Ko 19 B5
Biysk 18 D10
Black Forest = Schwarzwald 10 D5
Black Sea 15 F6
Black Volta → 30 C1
Blackburn 7 E5
Blackpool 7 E5
Blacksburg 42 G7
Blagoveshchensk 18 D14
Blanc, Mont 8 D7
Blantyre 33 H6
Blenheim 35 J13
Blitar 22 D3
Bloemfontein 31 B4
Bloemhof 31 B4
Blois 8 C4
Bloomington 42 F4
Bloomsburg 42 E9
Blue Mts., Oreg., U.S.A. 40 A3
Blue Mts., Pa., U.S.A. 42 E9
Blue Nile → 29 E11
Blue Ridge Mts. 41 C10
Bluefield 42 G7
Bobcaygeon 42 C8
Bobo-Dioulasso 28 F4
Bóbr → 10 B8
Bobruysk 11 B15
Bochum 10 C4
Boden 6 E12
Bodø 6 E10
Bodrog → 11 D11
Bogor 22 D2
Bogotá 46 B2
Bogra 23 G12
Bohemian Forest = Böhmerwald 10 D7
Böhmerwald 10 D7
Bohol 22 C4
Bohol Sea 22 C4
Boise 40 B3
Bolgatanga 30 B1
Bolivia ■ 46 D3
Bolivian Plateau 46 D3
Bologna 12 B4
Bolshevik I. 18 B12
Bolton 7 E5
Bolzano 12 A4
Boma 32 F2
Bombay 25 D6
Bonifacio 8 F8
Bonn 10 C4
Boonville 42 F4
Boothia, Gulf of 39 A11
Boothia Pen. 38 A10
Borås 6 G10
Bordeaux 8 D3
Borisov 11 A15
Borneo 22 C3
Bornholm 6 G11
Bosnia-Herzegovina ■ 12 B7
Bosporus 13 D13
Boston 43 D12
Bothnia, G. of 6 F12
Botletle → 31 A3
Botoşani 11 E14
Botswana ■ 31 A3
Bouaké 28 G3
Bouar 32 C3
Boulogne-sur-Mer 8 A4
Bourbonnais 8 C5
Bourg-en-Bresse 8 C6
Bourges 8 C5
Bourgogne 8 C6
Bourke 34 G8
Bournemouth 7 F6
Bowling Green, Ky., U.S.A. 42 G4
Bowling Green, Ohio, U.S.A. 42 E6
Bracebridge 42 C8
Bräcke 6 F11
Bradford, U.K. 7 E6
Bradford, U.S.A. 42 E8
Braga 9 B1
Brahmanbaria 23 H13
Brahmani → 23 J11
Brahmaputra → 23 H12
Brăila 11 F14
Brampton 42 D8
Brandenburg 10 B7
Brandenburg □ 10 B6
Brandon 38 D10
Brandvlei 31 C3
Brantford 42 D7
Bras d'Or, L. 43 C17
Brasília 46 D5
Braşov 11 F13
Brassey Ra. 22 C3
Bratislava 11 D9
Brattleboro 43 D11
Brazil 42 F4
Brazil ■ 46 D5
Brazzaville 32 E3
Breda 10 C3
Bredasdorp 31 C3
Bregenz 10 E5
Breiðafjörður 6 B2
Bremen 10 B5
Bremerhaven 10 B5
Brenner P. 10 E6
Bréscia 12 B4
Brest, Belarus 11 B12
Brest, France 8 B1
Bretagne 8 B2
Brewer 43 C13
Breyten 31 B4
Briançon 8 D7
Bridgeport 43 E11
Bridgeton 43 F10
Bridgetown 44 P22
Bridgewater 43 C15
Brighton 7 F6
Brindisi 13 D7
Brisbane 34 F9
Bristol 7 F5
Bristol Channel 7 F4
British Columbia □ 38 C7
British Isles 4 E5
Brits 31 B4
Britstown 31 C3
Brittany = Bretagne 8 B2
Brive-la-Gaillarde 8 D4
Brno 11 D9
Brocken 10 C6
Brockville 43 C10
Broken Hill 34 G7
Brooks Ra. 38 B5
Bruay-en-Artois 8 A5
Bruce, Mt. 34 E2
Brugge 10 C2
Brunei ■ 22 C3
Brunswick, Germany 10 B6
Brunswick, U.S.A. 43 D13
Brussels 10 C3
Bryan 42 E5
Bryansk 14 D5
Bucaramanga 46 B2
Bucharest 11 F14
Buckhannon 42 F7
Buckingham 43 C10
Bucyrus 42 E6
Budapest 11 E10
Buena Vista 42 G8
Buenos Aires 47 F4
Buffalo 42 D8
Bug → 11 B11
Buh → 15 E5
Bujumbura 32 E5
Bukavu 32 E5
Bukittinggi 22 D2
Bulandshahr 23 E6
Bulawayo 33 J5
Bulgaria ■ 13 C11
Bunbury 34 G2
Bundaberg 34 E9
Bundi 23 G5
Buraydah 24 C3
Burgas 13 C12
Burgersdorp 31 C4
Burgos 9 A4
Burgundy = Bourgogne 8 C6
Burkina Faso ■ 30 B1
Burlington, Vt., U.S.A. 43 C11
Burlington, Wis., U.S.A. 42 D3
Burlyu-Tyube 18 E9
Burma ■ 25 C8
Burnie 34 J8
Bursa 13 D13
Buru 22 D4
Burundi ■ 32 E5
Bushehr 24 C4
Butler 42 E8
Buton 22 D4
Butterworth 22 C2
Butuan 22 C4
Buzău 11 F14
Bydgoszcz 11 B9
Byelorussia = Belarus ■ 11 B14
Bytom 11 C10

Cabinda □ 32 F2
Cabonga, Réservoir 42 B9
Čačak 13 C9
Cáceres 9 C2
Cadillac 42 C5
Cádiz 9 D2
Caen 8 B3
Cagayan de Oro 22 C4
Cágliari 12 E3
Cahors 8 D4
Caicos Is. 45 C10
Cairns 34 D8
Cairo 29 B11
Calabar 30 D3
Calábria □ 12 E7
Calais, France 8 A4
Calais, U.S.A. 43 C14
Calamian Group 22 B3
Calapan 22 B4
Calcutta 23 H12
Caledon 31 C2
Caledon → 31 C4
Calgary 38 C8
Cali 46 B2
Calicut 25 D6
California □ 40 C2
California, G. of 44 B2
Calitzdorp 31 C3
Callao 46 D2
Caltanissetta 12 F6
Calvi 8 E8
Calvinia 31 C2
Camagüey 45 C9
Camargue 8 E6
Cambay, G. of 23 J4
Cambodia ■ 22 B2
Cambrai 8 A5
Cambrian Mts. 7 E5
Cambridge, U.K. 7 E7
Cambridge, Mass., U.S.A. 43 D12
Cambridge, Md., U.S.A. 43 F9
Cambridge, Ohio, U.S.A. 42 E7
Cambridge Bay 38 B9
Camden 43 F10
Cameroon ■ 30 C4
Cameroun, Mt. 30 D3
Campánia □ 12 D6
Campbellsville 42 G5
Campbellton 43 B14
Campeche 44 D6
Campeche, G. of 44 D6
Campina Grande 46 C6
Campinas 47 E5
Campo Grande 46 E4
Campos 46 E5
Camrose 38 C8
Can Tho 22 B2
Canada ■ 38 C10
Canadian Shield 39 C10
Canandaigua 42 D9
Canary Is. 28 C1
Canaveral, C. 41 E10
Canberra 34 H8
Cannes 8 E7
Canso 43 C17
Cantabria □ 9 A4
Cantabrian Mts. 9 A3
Canterbury 7 F7
Canton, N.Y., U.S.A. 43 C10
Canton, Ohio, U.S.A. 42 E7
Cap-Chat 43 A14
Cap-de-la-Madeleine 43 B11
Cape Breton I. 43 B17
Cape Charles 43 G10
Cape Coast 30 C1
Cape May 43 F10
Cape Town 31 C2
Cape Verde Is. ■ 27 E1
Cape York Peninsula 34 C7
Capreol 42 B7
Capri 12 D6
Caracas 46 A3
Carbondale 43 E10
Carcassonne 8 E5
Cardiff 7 F5
Caribbean Sea 45 E10
Caribou 43 B13
Carleton Place 43 C9
Carletonville 31 B4
Carlisle 42 E9
Carmaux 8 D5
Carmi 42 F3
Carnarvon, Australia 34 E1
Carnarvon, S. Africa 31 C3
Carnegie, L. 34 F3
Caro 42 D6
Carolina 31 B5
Caroline Is. 36 G6
Carpathians 11 D11
Carpentaria, G. of 34 C6
Carpentras 8 D6
Cartagena, Colombia 46 A2
Cartagena, Spain 9 D5
Casablanca 28 B3
Cascade Ra. 40 A2
Casper 40 B5
Caspian Sea 15 F9
Cass City 42 D6
Castellón de la Plana 9 C5
Castelsarrasin 8 E4
Castilla La Mancha □ 9 C4
Castilla y Leon □ 9 B3
Castres 8 E5
Castries 44 N21
Cataluña □ 9 B6
Catanduanes 22 B4
Catánia 12 F6
Catanzaro 12 E7
Catskill 43 D11
Catskill Mts. 43 D10
Caucasus Mountains 15 F7
Caxias do Sul 47 E4
Cayenne 46 B4
Cayuga L. 42 D9
Cedar Rapids 41 B8
Cegléd 11 E10
Celebes Sea 22 C4
Celina 42 E5
Central African Rep. ■ 32 C4
Central Makran Range 24 C5
Cephalonia = Kefallinía 13 E9
Ceram 22 D4
Ceram Sea 22 D4
Ceres 31 C2
Cerignola 12 D6
České Budějovice 10 D8
Ceuta 9 E3
Cévennes 8 D5
Chad ■ 29 E8
Chakradharpur 23 H10
Chaleur B. 43 B15
Chalisgaon 23 J5
Chalon-sur-Saône 8 C6
Châlons-en-Champagne 8 B6
Chamba 23 C6
Chambal → 23 F7
Chambersburg 42 F9
Chambéry 8 D6
Champagne 8 B6
Champaign 42 E3
Champlain, L. 43 C11
Chandigarh 23 D6
Chandpur 23 H13
Changchun 21 B7
Changde 21 D6
Changsha 21 D6
Changzhou 21 C6
Chanthaburi 22 B2
Chapleau 42 B6
Chapra 23 G10
Chardzhou 18 F8
Chārīkār 23 B2
Charleroi 10 C3
Charles, C. 43 G10
Charleston, Ill., U.S.A. 42 F3
Charleston, S.C., U.S.A. 41 D11
Charleston, W. Va., U.S.A. 42 F7
Charleville 34 F8
Charleville-Mézières 8 B6
Charlevoix 42 C5
Charlotte, Mich., U.S.A. 42 D5
Charlotte, N.C., U.S.A. 41 C10
Charlottesville 42 F8
Charlottetown 43 B16
Charolles 8 C6
Charters Towers 34 E8
Chartres 8 B4
Châteaubriant 8 C3
Châteaulin 8 B1
Châteauroux 8 C4
Châtellerault 8 C4
Chatham, N.B., Canada 43 B15
Chatham, Ont., Canada 42 D6
Chattanooga 41 C9
Chaumont 8 B6
Cheb 10 C7
Cheboksary 14 C8
Cheboygan 42 C5
Chechenia □ 15 F8
Chedabucto B. 43 C17
Chełm 11 C12
Chelyabinsk 18 D8
Chelyuskin, C. 18 B12
Chemnitz 10 C7
Chenab → 23 D3
Chengdu 20 C5
Chennai = Madras 25 D7
Cher → 8 C4
Cherbourg 8 B3
Cheremkhovo 18 D12
Cherepovets 14 C6
Cherkassy 15 E5
Chernigov 14 D5
Chernobyl 11 C16
Chernovtsy 11 D13
Cherski Ra. 18 C16
Chesapeake B. 42 F9
Chester 43 F10
Chesterfield Inlet 38 B10
Chesuncook L. 43 B13
Chhatarpur 23 G7
Chiai 21 D7
Chiba 19 B7
Chibougamau 43 A10
Chibougamau L. 43 A10
Chicago 42 E4
Chiclayo 46 C2
Chicopee 43 D11
Chicoutimi 43 A12
Chidley, C. 39 B13
Chieti 12 C6
Chihli, G. of 21 C6
Chihuahua 44 B3
Chile ■ 47 F2
Chilka L. 23 K10
Chillán 47 F2
Chillicothe 42 F6
Chilpancingo 44 D5
Chilton 42 C3
Chilung 21 D7
Chimborazo 46 C2
Chimbote 46 C2
Chimkent 18 E8
China ■ 21 C6
Chindwin → 25 C8
Chingola 33 G5
Chinon 8 C4
Chíos 13 E12
Chipata 33 G6
Chipman 43 B15
Chita 18 D13
Chitral 23 B3
Chittagong 23 H13
Cholet 8 C3
Chŏngjin 21 B7
Chongqing 20 D5
Chorzów 11 C10
Choybalsan 21 B6
Christchurch 35 J13
Christiana 31 B4
Chukot Ra. 18 C19
Chumphon 22 B1
Chur 10 E5
Churchill →, Man., Canada 38 C10
Churchill →, Nfld., Canada 39 C13
Churu 23 E5
Chushal 23 C7
Chuvashia □ 14 C8
Cicero 42 E4
Ciechanów 11 B11
Ciénaga 46 A2
Cienfuegos 45 C8
Cincinnati 42 F5
Cinto, Mte. 8 E8
Circleville 42 F6
Cirebon 22 D2
Citlaltépetl 44 D5
Ciudad Bolívar 46 B3
Ciudad Guayana 46 B3
Ciudad Juárez 44 A3
Ciudad Madero 44 C5
Ciudad Obregón 44 B3
Ciudad Real 9 C4
Ciudad Victoria 44 C5
Clanwilliam 31 C2
Claremont 43 D11
Clarksburg 42 F7
Clarksville 41 C9
Clearfield 42 E8
Clermont-Ferrand 8 D5
Cleveland 42 E7
Clifton Forge 42 G8
Cluj-Napoca 11 E12
Clyde → 7 D4
Coast Mts. 38 C7
Coast Ranges 40 B2
Coaticook 43 C12
Coatzacoalcos 44 D6
Cobourg 42 D8
Cochabamba 46 D3
Cochin 25 E6
Cochrane 42 A7
Cockburn I. 42 C6
Cod, C. 41 B13
Cognac 8 D3
Coimbatore 25 D6
Coimbra 9 B1
Colebrook 43 C12
Colesberg 31 C4
Colima 44 D4
Collingwood 42 C7
Colmar 8 B7
Cologne 10 C4
Colombia ■ 46 B2
Colombo 25 E6
Colón 44 H14
Colonial Heights 42 G9
Colorado □ 40 C5
Colorado →, N. Amer. 40 D4
Colorado →, U.S.A. 41 E7
Colorado Plateau 40 C4
Colorado Springs 40 C6
Columbia 41 D10
Columbia → 40 A2
Columbia, District of □ 42 F9
Columbus, Ga., U.S.A. 41 D10
Columbus, Ind., U.S.A. 42 F5
Columbus, Ohio, U.S.A. 42 F6
Comilla 23 H13
Communism Pk. 18 F9
Como 12 B3
Como, L. di 12 B3
Comodoro Rivadavia 47 G3
Comorin, C. 25 E6
Comoros ■ 27 H8
Compiègne 8 B5
Conakry 28 G2
Concepción 47 F2
Conchos → 44 B3
Concord 43 D12
Congo ■ 32 E3
Congo → 32 F2
Congo, Dem. Rep. of the ■ 32 E4
Coniston 42 B7
Conneaut 42 E7
Connecticut □ 43 E11
Connecticut → 43 E11
Connellsville 42 E8
Connersville 42 F5
Constance, L. 10 E5
Constanţa 11 F15
Constantine 28 A6
Conway 43 D12
Cook, Mt. 35 J13
Cook Is. 35 E17
Cook Strait 35 J13
Copenhagen 6 G10
Copper Harbor 42 B4
Coppermine 38 B8
Coppermine → 38 B8
Coral Sea 36 J7
Corbin 42 G5
Córdoba, Argentina 47 F3
Córdoba, Spain 9 D3
Cordova 38 B5
Corfu 13 E8
Corinth, G. of 13 E10
Cork 7 F2
Corner Brook 39 D14
Corning 42 D9
Cornwall 43 C10
Coromandel Coast 25 D7
Coronation Gulf 38 B8
Corpus Christi 40 E7
Corrientes 47 E4
Corry 42 E8
Corse, C. 8 E8
Corsica 8 F8
Corte 8 E8
Cortland 43 D9
Cosenza 12 E7
Coshocton 42 E7
Costa Blanca 9 C5
Costa Brava 9 B7
Costa del Sol 9 D3
Costa Dorada 9 B6
Costa Rica ■ 45 F8
Côte d'Azur 8 E7
Côte-d'Ivoire = Ivory Coast ■ 28 G3
Cotentin 8 B3
Cotonou 30 C2
Cotopaxi 46 C2
Cotswold Hills 7 F5
Cottbus 10 C8
Coudersport 42 E8
Council Bluffs 41 B7
Coventry 7 E6
Covington 42 F5
Cox's Bazar 23 J13
Cradock 31 C4
Craiova 11 F12
Cranbrook 38 D8
Crawfordsville 42 E4
Cremona 12 B4
Crete 13 G11
Creuse → 8 C4
Crimea 15 E5
Crişul Alb → 11 E11
Crişul Negru → 11 E11
Croatia ■ 10 F9
Crocodile → 31 B5
Crystal Falls 42 B3
Cuba ■ 45 C9
Cubango → 33 H4
Cúcuta 46 B2
Cuenca, Ecuador 46 C2
Cuenca, Spain 9 B4
Cuernavaca 44 D5
Cuiabá 46 D4
Culiacán 44 C3
Culpeper 42 F9
Cumberland 42 F8
Cumberland Plateau 41 C10
Cúneo 12 B2
Curitiba 47 E5
Cuttack 23 J10
Cuxhaven 10 B5
Cuyahoga Falls 42 E7
Cuzco 46 D2
Cyclades 13 F11
Cynthiana 42 F5
Cyprus ■ 24 B2
Czech Rep. ■ 10 D8
Częstochowa 11 C10

Da Nang 22 B2
Dacca 23 H13
Dadra and Nagar Haveli □ 23 J4
Dadu 23 F1
Dagestan □ 15 F8
Dagupan 22 B4
Dahod 23 H5
Dakar 28 F1
Dakhla 28 D1
Dalhousie 43 A14
Dalian 21 C7
Dallas 41 D7
Dalmatia 12 C7
Daloa 28 G3
Damaraland 31 A2

Taegu 21 C7
Taejon 21 C7
Taganrog 15 E6
Tagus → 9 C1
Tahiti 37 J13
Taibei 21 D7
Taichung 21 D7
Taimyr Peninsula 18 B11
Tainan 21 D7
Taiping 21 D7
Taiwan ■ 21 D7
Taiyuan 21 C6
Ta'izz 24 D3
Tajikistan ■ 18 F8
Tak 22 B1
Takamatsu 19 B4
Takaoka 19 A5
Takasaki 19 A6
Takla Makan 20 C3
Talaud Is. 22 C4
Talca 47 F2
Talcahuano 47 F2
Tallahassee 41 D10
Tallinn 14 C3
Tamale 30 C1
Tambov 14 D7
Tamil Nadu □ 25 D6
Tamo Abu Ra. 22 C3
Tampa 41 E10
Tampere 6 F12
Tampico 44 C5
Tamworth 34 G9
Tana → 6 D13
Tana, L. 29 F12
Tanami Desert 34 D5
Tananarive =
   Antananarivo 33 H9
Tando Adam 23 G2
Tanga 32 F7
Tanganyika, L. 32 F6
Tangier 28 A3
Tangshan 21 C6
Tanimbar Is. 22 D5
Tanjungbalai 22 C1
Tanzania ■ 32 F6
Tapajós → 46 C4
Tapi → 23 J4
Tappahannock 42 G9
Tarābulus, Lebanon 24 B2
Tarābulus, Libya 29 B7
Tarakan 22 C3
Táranto 12 D7
Táranto, G. di 12 D7
Tarbagatai Ra. 18 E10
Tarbes 8 E4
Tarim Basin 20 B3
Tarkastad 31 C4
Tarn → 8 E4
Tarnów 11 C11
Tarragona 9 B6
Tarrasa 9 B7
Tashkent 18 E8
Tasman Sea 35 L8
Tasmania □ 34 J8
Tatarsk 18 D9
Tatarstan □ 14 C9
Tatra 11 D11
Tatta 23 G1
Tauern 10 E7
Taung 31 B3
Taunton 43 E12
Taunus 10 C5
Taurus Mts. 15 G5
Tawas City 42 C6
Tawau 22 C3
Tbilisi 15 F7
Tchad, L. 29 F7
Tebingtinggi 22 C1
Tegal 22 D2
Tegucigalpa 44 E7
Tehran 24 B4
Tehuantepec, Gulf of 44 D5
Tehuantepec, Isthmus of 44 D6
Tel Aviv-Jaffa 24 B2
Tell City 42 G4
Telukbutun 22 C2
Tema 30 C2
Temba 31 B4
Témiscaming 42 B8
Tenerife 28 C1
Tennessee □ 41 C9
Tennessee → 41 C9
Tepic 44 C4
Téramo 12 C5
Teresina 46 C5
Ternate 22 C4
Terni 12 C5
Ternopol 11 D13
Terre Haute 42 F4
Teruel 9 B5
Tetouan 28 A3
Tetovo 13 C9
Teutoburger Wald 10 B5
Texas □ 40 D7
Texel 10 B3
Tezpur 23 F14
Thabana Ntlenyana 31 B4
Thabazimbi 31 A4
Thailand ■ 22 B2

Thailand, G. of 22 B2
Thal 23 C3
Thal Desert 23 D3
Thames →, Canada 42 D6
Thames →, U.K. 7 F7
Thane 23 K4
Thar Desert 23 E4
The Hague 10 B3
The Pas 38 C9
Thessalon 42 B6
Thessaloniki 13 D10
Thessaloniki, Gulf of 13 D10
Thetford Mines 43 B12
Thiers 8 D5
Thies 28 F1
Thimphu 23 F12
Thionville 8 B7
Thunder B. 42 C6
Thunder Bay 42 A3
Thüringer Wald 10 C6
Tian Shan 20 B3
Tianjin 21 C6
Tianshui 20 C5
Tiber → 12 D5
Tibesti 29 D8
Tibet □ 20 C3
Ticino → 12 B3
Ticonderoga 43 D11
Tierra del Fuego 47 H3
Tiffin 42 E6
Tignish 43 B15
Tigris → 24 B3
Tijuana 44 A1
Tiksi 18 B14
Tilburg 10 C3
Timaru 35 J13
Timiṣoara 11 F11
Timmins 42 A7
Timor 22 D4
Tinaca Pt. 22 C4
Tirana 13 D8
Tiraspol 11 E15
Tîrgoviṣte 11 F13
Tîrgu-Jiu 11 F12
Tîrgu Mureṣ 11 E13
Tirich Mir 23 A3
Tirol □ 10 E6
Tiruchchirappalli 25 D6
Tirunelveli 25 E6
Tisa → 13 B9
Titicaca, L. 46 D3
Titusville 42 E8
Tizi-Ouzou 28 A5
Toamasina 33 H9
Toba Kakar 23 D2
Tobago 44 S20
Tobermory 42 C7
Tocantins → 46 C5
Togliatti 14 D8
Togo ■ 30 C2
Tokelau Is. 35 B16
Tōkyō 19 B6
Toledo, Spain 9 C3
Toledo, U.S.A. 42 E6
Toliara 33 J8
Toluca 44 D5
Tomaszów Mazowiecki 11 C10
Tombouctou 30 A1
Tomini, G. of 22 D4
Tomsk 18 D10
Tonga ■ 35 D16
Tonga Trench 35 E16
Tongaat 31 B5
Tongking, G. of 20 E5
Tonk 23 F5
Tonlé Sap 22 B2
Toowoomba 34 F9
Topeka 41 C7
Torne → 6 E12
Torne, L. 6 E11
Tornio 6 E12
Toronto 42 D8
Torre del Greco 12 D6
Torreón 44 B4
Tortosa 9 B6
Toruń 11 B10
Toscana □ 12 C4
Toteng 31 A3
Toul 8 B6
Toulon 8 E6
Toulouse 8 E4
Touraine 8 C4
Tournai 10 C2
Tournon 8 D6
Tours 8 C4
Touwsrivier 31 C3
Towanda 42 E9
Townsville 34 D8
Towson 42 F9
Toyama 19 A5
Toyohashi 19 B5
Trabzon 15 F6
Trafalgar, C. 9 D2
Trail 38 D8
Trang 22 C1
Trangan 22 D5
Transantarctic Mts. 48 F16

Transylvania 11 E12
Transylvanian Alps 11 F13
Trápani 12 E5
Traverse City 42 C5
Trento 12 A4
Trenton, Canada 42 C9
Trenton, U.S.A. 43 E10
Trier 10 D4
Trieste 12 B5
Trincomalee 25 E7
Trinidad & Tobago ■ 44 S20
Tripura □ 23 H13
Trivandrum 25 E6
Trnava 11 D9
Trois-Rivières 43 B11
Trollhättan 6 G10
Trondheim 6 F10
Trondheim Fjord 6 F10
Troy, N.Y., U.S.A. 43 D11
Troy, Ohio, U.S.A. 42 E5
Troyes 8 B6
Trujillo 46 C2
Truk 36 G7
Truro 43 C16
Tsau 31 A3
Tshabong 31 B3
Tshane 31 A3
Tshwane 31 A3
Tsimlyansk Res. 15 E7
Tsu 19 B5
Tsumeb 31 A2
Tsumis 31 A2
Tuamotu Arch. 37 J13
Tubuai Is. 37 K12
Tucson 40 D4
Tugela → 31 B5
Tula 14 D6
Tulcea 11 F15
Tulle 8 D4
Tulsa 41 C7
Tunis 28 A7
Tunisia ■ 28 B6
Tunja 46 B2
Tura 23 G13
Turabah 24 C3
Turin 12 B2
Turkana, L. 32 D7
Turkey ■ 15 G6
Turkmenistan ■ 18 F7
Turks & Caicos Is. ■ 45 C10
Turku 6 F12
Tuscany = Toscana □ 12 C4
Tuticorin 25 E6
Tuvalu ■ 35 B14
Tuxtla Gutiérrez 44 D6
Tuz Gölü 15 G5
Tuzla 13 B8
Tver 14 C6
Two Rivers 42 C4
Tychy 11 C10
Tyrol = Tirol □ 10 E6
Tyrrhenian Sea 12 E5
Tyumen 18 D8
Tzaneen 31 A5

U.S.A. = United States of America ■ 40 C7
Ubangi = Oubangi → 32 E3
Ube 19 C2
Uberaba 46 D5
Uberlândia 46 D5
Ucayali → 46 C2
Udaipur 23 G4
Udaipur Garhi 23 F11
Údine 12 A5
Udmurtia □ 14 C9
Udon Thani 22 B2
Ufa 14 D10
Uganda ■ 32 D6
Uitenhage 31 C4
Ujjain 23 H5
Ujung Pandang 22 D3
Ukraine ■ 15 E5
Ulan Bator 20 B5
Ulan Ude 18 D12
Ulhasnagar 23 K4
Ulm 10 D5
Ulyasutay 20 B4
Ume → 6 F12
Umeå 6 F12
Umtata 31 C4
Umzimvubu 31 C4
Umzinto 31 C5
Ungava B. 39 C13
Ungava Pen. 39 C12
Uniontown 42 F8
United Arab Emirates ■ 24 C4
United Kingdom ■ 7 E6
United States of America ■ 40 C7
Upington 31 B3
Uppsala 6 G11
Ural → 15 E9
Ural Mts. 14 C10
Uralsk 14 D9

Uranium City 38 C9
Urbana, Ill., U.S.A. 42 E3
Urbana, Ohio, U.S.A. 42 E6
Urmia, L. 24 B3
Uruguay ■ 47 F4
Uruguay → 47 F4
Ürümqi 20 B3
Usakos 31 A2
Ushant 8 B1
Ust Urt Plateau 18 E7
Ústí nad Labem 10 C8
Utah □ 40 C4
Utica 43 D10
Utrecht 10 B3
Utsunomiya 19 A6
Uttar Pradesh □ 23 F8
Uttaradit 22 B2
Uusikaupunki 6 F12
Uzbekistan ■ 18 E8
Uzhhorod 11 D12

Vaal → 31 B3
Vaal Dam 31 B4
Vaasa 6 F12
Vadodara 23 H4
Vadso 6 D13
Vaduz 10 E5
Val d'Or 42 A9
Valahia 11 F13
Valdés, Pen. 47 E3
Valdez 38 B5
Valdivia 47 F2
Valence 8 D6
Valencia, Spain 9 C5
Valencia, Venezuela 46 A3
Valenciennes 8 A5
Valladolid 9 B3
Valletta 12 G6
Valparaíso 47 F2
Van, L. 15 G7
Van Buren 43 B13
Van Wert 42 E5
Vancouver 38 D7
Vancouver I. 38 D7
Vanderbijlpark 31 B4
Vanderkloof Dam 31 C3
Vänern 6 G10
Vännäs 6 F11
Vannes 8 C2
Vanrhynsdorp 31 C2
Vanua Levu 35 D14
Vanuatu ■ 35 D12
Varanasi 23 G9
Varanger Fjord 6 D13
Varberg 6 G10
Varna 13 C12
Västerås 6 G11
Västervik 6 G11
Vatican City ■ 12 D5
Vatnajökull 6 B5
Vättern 6 G10
Vega 6 E10
Vellore 25 D6
Vendée □ 8 C3
Vendôme 8 C4
Venezuela ■ 46 B3
Venice 12 B5
Ventoux, Mt. 8 D6
Veracruz 44 D5
Veraval 23 J3
Vercelli 12 B3
Verdun 8 B6
Vereeniging 31 B4
Verkhoyansk 18 C15
Verkhoyansk Ra. 18 C14
Vermont □ 43 D11
Verona 12 B4
Versailles 8 B5
Verviers 10 C3
Vesoul 8 C7
Vesterålen 6 E10
Vesuvio 12 D6
Veszprém 11 E9
Vicenza 12 B4
Vichy 8 C5
Victoria 38 D7
Victoria □ 34 H7
Victoria, L. 32 E6
Victoria de Durango 44 C4
Victoria Falls 33 H5
Victoria I. 38 A8
Victoria West 31 C3
Victoriaville 43 B12
Vienna 10 D9
Vienne 8 D6
Vienne → 8 C4
Vientiane 22 B2
Vierzon 8 C5
Vigo 9 A1
Vijayawada 25 D7
Vikna 6 F10
Vilaine → 8 C2
Vilhelmina 6 F11
Villach 10 E7
Villahermosa 44 D6
Ville-Marie 42 B8

Villeneuve-sur-Lot 8 D4
Vilnius 14 D4
Vilyuy → 18 C14
Vilyuysk 18 C14
Viña del Mar 47 F2
Vincennes 42 F4
Vindhya Ra. 23 H6
Vineland 43 F10
Vinnitsa 11 D15
Vire 8 B3
Virgin Is. (British) ■ 45 D12
Virgin Is. (U.S.) ■ 45 D12
Virginia 31 B4
Virginia □ 42 G8
Visby 6 G11
Vishakhapatnam 25 D7
Viterbo 12 C5
Viti Levu 35 D14
Vitória, Brazil 46 E5
Vitoria, Spain 9 A4
Vitsyebsk 14 C5
Vladikavkaz 15 F7
Vladimir 14 C7
Vladivostok 18 E15
Vlissingen 10 C2
Vlóra 13 D8
Vltava → 10 D8
Vogelkop 22 D5
Vogelsberg 10 C5
Vojvodina □ 13 B9
Volga → 15 E8
Volga Hts. 15 D8
Volgograd 15 E7
Volksrust 31 B4
Vologda 14 C6
Vólos 13 E10
Volta → 30 C2
Volta, L. 30 C2
Volzhskiy 15 E7
Voronezh 14 D6
Vorkuta 14 A11
Vosges 8 B7
Vrede 31 B4
Vredenburg 31 C2
Vryburg 31 B3
Vryheid 31 B5
Vyatka → 14 C9

Waal → 10 C3
Wabash 42 E5
Wabash → 42 G3
Waco 41 D7
Wâd Medanî 29 F11
Waddington, Mt. 38 C7
Wagga Wagga 34 H8
Wah 23 C4
Waigeo 22 D5
Wainganga → 23 K7
Waingapu 22 D4
Wakayama 19 B4
Wales □ 7 E5
Walgett 34 F8
Wallaceburg 42 D6
Wallachia = Valahia 11 F13
Wallis & Futuna, Is. 35 C15
Walvis Bay 31 A1
Wanganui 35 H14
Wapakoneta 42 E5
Warangal 25 D6
Wardha → 23 K7
Warmbad 31 A4
Warrego → 34 G7
Warren, Mich., U.S.A. 42 D6
Warren, Ohio, U.S.A. 42 E7
Warren, Pa., U.S.A. 42 E8
Warrenton 31 B3
Warrnambool 34 H7
Warsaw, Poland 11 B11
Warsaw, U.S.A. 42 E5
Warta → 11 B9
Warwick 43 E12
Wasatch Ra. 40 B4
Washington, D.C., U.S.A. 42 F9
Washington, Ind., U.S.A. 42 F4
Washington, Pa., U.S.A. 42 E7
Washington □ 40 A2
Washington, Mt. 43 C12
Washington I. 42 C4
Waterbury 43 E11
Waterford 7 E3
Waterloo 42 D7
Watertown 43 D10
Waterval-Boven 31 B5
Waterville 43 C13
Watseka 42 E4
Watubela Is. 22 D5
Waukegan 42 D4
Waukesha 42 D3
Wauwatosa 42 D4
Wawa 42 B5

Wayne 42 F6
Waynesboro 42 F8
Waynesburg 42 F7
Wazirabad 23 C5
Webster Springs 42 F7
Weddell Sea 48 E5
Weifang 21 C6
Welch 42 G7
Welkom 31 B4
Welland 42 D8
Wellesley Is. 34 D6
Wellington 35 J13
Wellsboro 42 E9
Wellsville 42 D9
Wels 10 D8
Wenzhou 21 D7
Wepener 31 B4
Weser → 10 B5
West Bend 42 D3
West Bengal □ 23 H11
West Beskids 11 D10
West Fjord 6 E10
West Point 42 G9
West Pt. 43 A15
West Virginia □ 42 F7
Westbrook 43 D12
Western Australia □ 34 F3
Western Ghats 25 D6
Western Sahara ■ 28 D2
Western Samoa ■ 35 C16
Westerwald 10 C4
Westminster 42 F9
Weston 42 F7
Wetar 22 D4
Whangarei 35 H13
Wheeling 42 E7
White → 42 F4
White Nile → 29 E11
White Sea 14 A6
Whitefish Point 42 B5
Whitehorse 38 B6
Whitewater 42 D3
Whitney, Mt. 40 C3
Whyalla 34 G6
Wiarton 42 C7
Wichita 41 C7
Wichita Falls 40 D7
Wiener Neustadt 10 E9
Wiesbaden 10 C5
Wilge → 31 B4
Wilhelmshaven 10 B5
Wilkes-Barre 43 E10
Willemstad 45 E11
Williamsburg 42 G9
Williamson 42 G6
Williamsport 42 E9
Williston 41 C3
Willowmore 31 C3
Wilmington, Del., U.S.A. 43 F10
Wilmington, Ohio, U.S.A. 42 F6
Winchester, Ky., U.S.A. 42 G6
Winchester, Va., U.S.A. 42 F8
Windhoek 31 A2
Windsor 42 D6
Windward Is. 44 P20
Winnebago, L. 42 D3
Winnipeg 38 D10
Winnipeg, L. 38 C10
Winooski 43 C11
Winston-Salem 41 C10
Winterthur 10 E5
Wisconsin □ 41 B9
Witbank 31 B4
Witdraai 31 B3
Wkra → 11 B11
Włocławek 11 B10
Wokam 22 D5
Wolfsburg 10 B6
Wollongong 34 G9
Wolverhampton 7 E5
Wönsan 21 C7
Woods, L. of the 38 D10
Woodstock 42 D7
Woonsocket 43 E11
Worcester, S. Africa 31 C2
Worcester, U.S.A. 43 D12
Worms 10 D5
Wrangel I. 18 B19
Wrocław 11 C9
Wuhan 21 C6
Wuhu 21 C6
Wuppertal 10 C4
Würzburg 10 D5
Wutongqiao 20 D5
Wuxi 21 C7
Wuzhou 21 D6
Wyndham 34 D4
Wyoming □ 40 B5

Xau, L. 31 A3
Xenia 42 F6
Xiaguan 20 D5
Xiamen 21 D6
Xi'an 21 C5
Xiangfan 21 C6

Xiangtan 21 D6
Xingu → 46 C4
Xining 20 C5
Xuzhou 21 C6

Yablonovyy Ra. 18 D13
Yakutsk 18 C14
Yamagata 19 A7
Yambol 13 C12
Yamdena 22 D5
Yamethin 25 C8
Yamuna → 23 G8
Yangtze Kiang → 21 C7
Yanji 21 B7
Yantai 21 C7
Yaoundé 30 D4
Yapen 22 D5
Yarkhun → 23 A4
Yarmouth 43 D14
Yaroslavl 14 C6
Yatsushiro 19 C2
Yazd 24 B4
Yekaterinburg 14 C11
Yellow Sea 21 C7
Yellowknife 38 B8
Yellowstone → 40 A6
Yellowstone National Park 40 B5
Yemen ■ 24 D3
Yenbo 24 C2
Yenisey → 18 B10
Yeniseysk 18 D11
Yeola 19 J5
Yerevan 15 F7
Yeu, I. d' 8 C2
Yibin 20 D5
Yichang 21 C6
Yining 20 B3
Yogyakarta 22 D3
Yokkaichi 19 B5
Yokohama 19 B6
Yokosuka 19 B6
Yonkers 43 E11
Yonne → 8 B5
York, U.K. 7 E6
York, U.S.A. 42 F9
Yosemite National Park 40 C3
Yoshkar Ola 14 C8
Youngstown 42 E7
Yuan Jiang → 21 D6
Yucatan 44 D7
Yucatan Str. 44 C7
Yugoslavia ■ 13 B9
Yukon → 38 B3
Yukon Territory □ 38 B6
Yunnan □ 20 D5
Yuzhno-Sakhalinsk 18 E16
Yvetot 8 B4

Zabrze 11 C10
Zagreb 10 F9
Zagros Mts. 24 B3
Zahedan 24 C5
Zaïre = Congo, Dem. Rep. of the ■ 32 E4
Zaïre = Congo → 32 F2
Zákinthos 13 F9
Zambezi → 33 H7
Zambia ■ 33 G5
Zamboanga 22 C4
Zamora 9 B3
Zamość 11 C12
Zanesville 42 F6
Zanjan 24 B3
Zanzibar 32 F7
Zaporozhye 15 E6
Zaragoza 9 B5
Zaria 30 B3
Zaskar Mts. 23 C6
Zeebrugge 10 C2
Zeerust 31 B4
Zenica 13 B7
Zhangjiakou 21 B6
Zhangzhou 21 D6
Zhanjiang 21 D6
Zhejiang □ 21 D7
Zhengzhou 21 C6
Zhigansk 18 C14
Zhitomir 11 C15
Zibo 21 C6
Zielona Góra 10 C8
Zigong 20 D5
Ziguinchor 28 F1
Žilina 11 D10
Zimbabwe ■ 33 H5
Zion National Park 40 C4
Zlatoust 14 C10
Zlin 11 D9
Zonguldak 15 F5
Zrenjanin 13 B9
Zug 10 E5
Zunyi 20 D5
Zürich 10 E5
Zwickau 10 C7
Zwolle 10 B4